TOWARDS VISITOR IMPACT MANAGEMENT

To our families

Towards Visitor Impact Management

Visitor Impacts, Carrying Capacity and Management
Responses in Europe's Historic Towns and Cities

JOHN GLASSON, KERRY GODFREY AND BRIAN GOODEY
Oxford Brookes University, UK

with
HELEN ABSALOM
ENTEC, Shankland Cox, UK
JAN VAN DER BORG
University of Venice, Italy

Ashgate

Published by
Ashgate Publishing Limited
Gower House
Croft Road
Aldershot
Hants GU11 3HR
England

Ashgate Publishing Company
131 Main Street
Burlington,
Vermont 05401-5600
USA

Ashgate website:http://www.ashgate.com

Reprinted 1997, 1999, 2000, 2002

British Library Cataloguing in Publication Data
Glasson, John
    Towards Vistor Impact Management:
    Vistor Impacts, Carrying Capacity and
    Management Responses in Europe's
    Historic Towns and Cities
    I. Title
    338.47914

Library of Congress Catalog Card Number: 95-78516

Typeset by
Carol Glasson
35 Quarry Road
Headington
Oxford OX3 8NU

ISBN 1 85972 054 4

Printed and bound in Great Britain by Biddles Limited,
Guildford and King's Lynn.

Contents

List of figures

The authors

John Glasson is Professor and Head of the School of Planning at Oxford Brookes University, and Research Director of the Impacts Assessment Unit in the School.

Kerry Godfrey is a Lecturer in Tourism Development in the School of Planning at Oxford Brookes University.

Brian Goodey is Professor in Urban Landscape Design in the Joint Centre for Urban Design, in the Schools of Architecture and Planning at Oxford Brookes University.

All three are members also of the Oxford Centre for Tourism and Leisure Studies (OCTALS) at Oxford Brookes University.

Helen Absalom is a Senior Consultant for ENTEC Shankland Cox, Kenilworth, UK.

Jan Van der Borg is a Lecturer in the International Centre of Studies on the Tourist Economy (CISET) in the University of Venice.

Preface and acknowledgements

As Europe's historic towns and cities came under increasing pressure from visitor numbers, the development of approaches to the better management of the visitor flows and their resultant impacts on the host environments becomes a matter of some urgency. Tourism can destroy tourism. The European Commission's Tourism and Environment research programme of the early 1990s provided an opportunity for some comparative work, learning from approaches and experiences across Europe's historic towns and cities. A particular focus of the work has been an exploration of the role of the carrying capacity of destinations and/or capacity limits. The achievement of a more sustainable tourism depends, in part, on a better understanding of the nature and dimensions of this elusive concept.

The book should provide a valuable text for undergraduate and postgraduate students in tourism, planning, environmental studies, geography and other built environment areas, including architecture, estate management, conservation and heritage studies. It should also be of value to practitioners in the field, including planners, developers, consultants, those in the many branches of the tourism industry, and local and national environmental interest groups. The Europe-wide comparative approach provides a text of relevance not only in Britain, but in the wider mainland of Europe and beyond.

Our grateful thanks are due to many people without whose help this book would not have been produced. We are particularly grateful to Carol Glasson who typed and retyped the original report, and has subsequently type set this book. Our thanks go to the European Commission for support for the initial study, especially to Richard Dickinson in the Tourism Unit of DG23; and to Michael Welbank for his help in the early stages of the research. We also wish to thank the many respondents to our Europe-wide questionnaire survey, and in particular those who participated in the Bruges Workshop.

1 Introduction

1.1 Introduction

Europe's heritage cities are coming under growing pressure from visitor numbers. With the increase in tourism in absolute terms, and with some shift from sand, sun and sea holidays to more heritage and cultural industry based holidays, this pressure is likely to become even more intense. By way of example, the British Tourist Authority invested in a major marketing campaign to promote 1995 as the 'Festival of Arts and Culture in Britain'. The importance of local action in the area of heritage and cultural tourism was noted in the 'Community Action Plan to Assist Tourism' (CEC, 1991). In the United Kingdom, the visitor-environment conflict in historic towns and cities was highlighted in the English Tourist Board/Department of Employment reports on 'Tourism and the Environment: Maintaining the Balance' (ETB, 1991), and in the major international conference in London in November 1992 on 'Tourism and the Environment: Challenges and Choices for the 1990s' (ETB/Department of National Heritage, 1993).

The development of approaches to the management of facilities and of areas visited by tourists raises the important concept of the carrying capacity of destinations and/or capacity limits. The achievement of a more sustainable tourism will depend, in part, on a better understanding of the nature and dimensions of this elusive concept. Yet there is little consensus, and this book seeks to draw together experience and innovative work from across Europe to better inform the management of the growing pressure of visitor numbers on our heritage cities. It draws on research undertaken in 1992 and 1993 by Oxford Brookes University, the University of Venice and Shankland Cox Environmental Planning, for the Tourism and Environment Programme of the Tourism Unit, Directorate General 23, of the Commission of the European

Union (CEU). Further sections of this first chapter now provide an outline context for the studies, clarify the objectives and research methods used, and outline the structure of the text.

1.2 Context

A large proportion of tourist activity in Europe utilises, or exploits, heritage in some manner or another, whether it be in visiting old buildings, museums, historic urban cities, towns or urban quarters, countryside landscapes, or natural sites. Often, these tourism components have great fragility or a susceptibility to damage if tourist numbers or values increase unchecked. Heritage components cannot easily be expanded and in most cases, are difficult and/or expensive to renew. In many cases, the heritage component is a non-renewable resource which, once destroyed, is lost forever.

The impacts of visitor numbers on heritage cities can take many forms and they can be analysed in various ways, including adverse/beneficial, short term/long term and reversible/irreversible. The development of environmental impact assessment (EIA) procedures and methods has helped to progress such analysis. A standard, simple, classification of tourism impacts would identify physical, social, economic and political *dimensions*. Physical impacts usually involve impacts on the natural and built environment; social impacts involve changes in the quality of life (including cultural changes) of the visitors and their hosts; economic impacts involve the economic costs and benefits to the various parties involved. Political impacts are less frequently discussed, but involve the decision making processes, policy formulation and implementation, which can be crucial in generating a management approach to the pressures of visitor numbers. Impacts also vary according to the perspective of the participant. The *perspectives* of the visitor, the local community, and of tourism policy decision makers are crucial in the exploration of the carrying capacity concept and in the visitor management responses.

Carrying capacity and visitor management are interrelated. Capacities of heritage cities and components within them are rarely absolute; they vary according to perception, and to management measures. Thus a better understanding of capacity issues, and of management responses, is important for several reasons, including:
(i)   safety and security of the heritage component itself;
(ii)   protection of the quality of the environment around the heritage component;
(iii)   enhancement of the visitor experience and visitor enjoyment;
(iv)   maintenance and, where possible, enhancement of the quality of life of the resident population; and

2

(v)   maintenance of the long term attraction and commercial viability of the destination.

1.3   Study objectives and target groups

Objectives of the study

The original objectives of the European Commission research project were as follows:
(i)   To review, develop and apply techniques of establishing carrying capacity which seek to accommodate:
  (a)   the quality of the tourist experience <u>and</u> the quality of the life of the resident population, and
  (b)   the various dimensions (physical infrastructure/environment/local economy/social) of capacity.
(ii)   To relate the study particularly to a range of attractions, which are components of cultural heritage, from small city to individual facility.
(iii) To test capacity approaches across a number of locations in north and south Europe, to assess their general and wider value, replicability, and to identify any location specific variables.
(iv)   To relate the results of the study to planning guidance and concepts for managing carrying capacity. The study also sought to identify where further work needed to be undertaken on guidance and management.
(v)   To spread good practice and uniform methods of approach within the European Union, and to exert a significant multiplier effect across several Member States and beyond (ie. Central and Eastern Europe).
(vi)   To provide a much needed methodology with easily applied tools which can be adopted by urban administrations for the management and development of their heritage resources. These were expected to include:
  (a)   methods for establishing capacities and for the regular monitoring of shifts in capacity at various levels in historic cities; and
  (b)   initial development of methods for positive management of visitor flows (including the introduction of intervening attractions and facilities more appropriate to established capacities).
The experience of the study substantially modified some of these objectives. As will be seen, the flexibility of the carrying capacity concept and the wide range of heritage city/site locations/attractions, requires a variety of responses in terms of methodology and management approaches.

3

Figure 1.1 Stages of the research programme

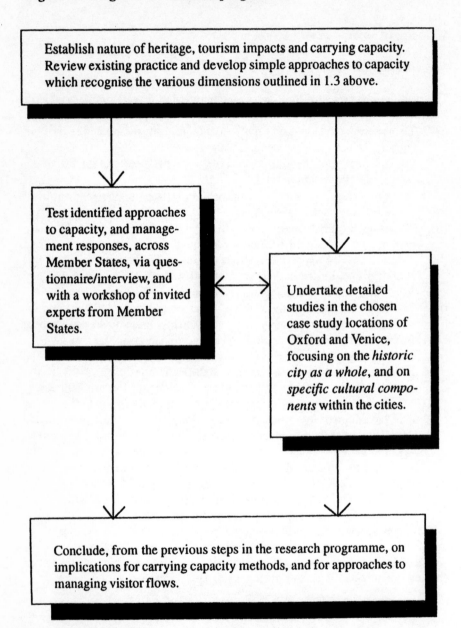

Establish nature of heritage, tourism impacts and carrying capacity. Review existing practice and develop simple approaches to capacity which recognise the various dimensions outlined in 1.3 above.

Test identified approaches to capacity, and management responses, across Member States, via questionnaire/interview, and with a workshop of invited experts from Member States.

Undertake detailed studies in the chosen case study locations of Oxford and Venice, focusing on the *historic city as a whole*, and on *specific cultural components* within the cities.

Conclude, from the previous steps in the research programme, on implications for carrying capacity methods, and for approaches to managing visitor flows.

Target groups

The target groups for the study are the local authorities, tourism board managers and planners responsible for the small and medium sized historic towns and cities in the Member States of the European Union. In many such centres the urban heritage draws tourists in such numbers as to create real or potential pressures between tourism, the environment and local residents. The research has sought to involve relevant centres in most Member States, and in non-Member States, including the newly emerging democracies of Eastern Europe.

Oxford (UK) and Venice (Italy) have been used as two centres for detailed study, and as examples of cities with intensive visitor pressures and evolving management approaches. The Oxford Visitor Study produced at the Oxford Centre for Tourism and Leisure Studies at Oxford Brookes University (Glasson *et al*, 1992) provided an important data base and starting point for the Oxford Study. Work on capacity studies by the School of Tourism Economics and Management at the University of Venice (Canestrelli and Costa, 1991; Costa and Van der Borg, 1991) provided innovative and detailed quantitative background studies for Venice.

1.4   Methods

The reserch programme included the four main stages illustrated in Figure 1.1. The first stage involved an investigation of the nature of the key elements in the research: heritage, impacts and carrying capacity. For the latter, the focus is on approaches which recognise the various dimensions of capacity (physical, social etc.), the various 'actor' perspectives (tourist, local resident etc.), and the need for workable and simple approaches, as a first step towards the more effective management of visitor flows.

The second stage involved an investigation of the nature of tourism pressures, resultant impacts, considerations of capacity limits, management responses and policy effectiveness, across a range of medium sized historic centres in EU Member States, and non-Member States in Europe. A questionnaire (see Appendix 1) was completed by respondents in over 100 historic cities, giving a unique overview of the perception of, and responses to, the problems associated with visitor numbers in historic centres in almost every country in Europe. As a follow-up to the questionnaire survey, a workshop was held in Bruges (Belgium), in September 1993, to provide more detailed studies of a cross section of the survey respondents. Presentations were made by participants from Bruges (Belgium), Helsingor (Denmark),

Chartres (France), Canterbury (UK), and Coimbra (Portugal), as well as from Venice and Oxford.

The third stage involved the detailed case studies of Venice and Oxford. Parallel studies were assembled on social and economic impacts and approaches to capacity, and on visitor and local resident perceptions of capacity issues. In addition, the Venice case study exemplifies the use and potential of a quantitative linear programming approach to defining capacity limits. In contrast to this 'hard' quantitative approach, the Oxford case study includes an additional study of the important 'softer' qualitative political dimension to capacity, via a survey of the members of the Oxford Tourism Forum. The Oxford case study also includes a number of more detailed site specific case studies; these were used to test the variations in impacts and management responses at a more localised scale than the city as a whole. In both the Oxford and Venice case studies, there was an examination of recent, current and planned approaches to visitor management.

The final stage brought together the findings from the various programme components. These findings are summarised in this text. The book also includes some subsequent work on relevant concepts, and on the case studies.

1.5   Structure of the book

Following this initial chapter, the structure of the book broadly parallels the stages of the programme outlined in Section 1.4. Chapters 2, 3 and 4 provide an overview and introduction to the nature of the urban identity, heritage and cultural industries (Chapter 2), which draw visitors to Europe's historic towns and cities in increasing numbers and generates a wide range of tourism impacts (Chapter 3), which raise issues of approaches to carrying capacity, limits to acceptable change, and visitor impact management (Chapter 4). Chapter 5 introduces the major Europe-wide questionnaire survey. The structure of the survey was derived from some of the concepts noted in Chapters 2, 3 and 4 and on management responses used in Oxford, Venice and elsewhere. The survey produced a wealth of data; only the key findings are included in Chapter 5. The following Chapter, 6, highlights impact issues, capacity considerations and management responses identified for a set of historic towns and cities used in the Bruges workshop and in follow-up studies. These have been amplified, as appropriate, with relevant points from reports produced for other cities and by invited participants who were unable to attend the Bruges workshop; documentation from Chester (UK), Salzburg (Austria) and Heidelberg (Germany) is of particular value. Chapters 7 and 8 provide the detailed case studies of Venice and Oxford. The final Chapter, 9, draws together some conclusions, including: *the importance of understanding the*

6

tourism pressures in particular historic towns and cities, the *flexibility of the carrying capacity concept, the importance of key strategic choices* and *alternative methods for visitor management,* examples of *good practice in visitor management* in a number of policy areas, and the need for an *integrated approach.*

2 Urban identity, heritage and the cultural industries

2.1 Introduction

Visiting cities is hardly a novel phenomenon. Urban places have relied on visitors for their development and economic survival. The use of public spaces and places for events, gatherings and selling is equally ancient. What is significant for this study is the relationship between these urban traditions, the spaces which they use, and the recent development of mass urban tourism, which has placed unprecedented pressures on historic city centres (Vetter, 1985). In order to understand both the problem, and the elements of a solution, we need to picture the evolution of the city, and the broader issues which surround its use at the close of the 20th century.

2.2 The city past

The emergence of each town and city has depended, in part at least, on those local factors of geography and culture which are now cited as the basis for *local and regional identity*. Waterside developments, outlooks borne of defensive origins, and locations central to a culture are common. The specific articulation of these within local topography gives each city its most enduring characteristics - Paris on the Seine, Edinburgh's dominant castle-topped rock, Bilbao as a focus for Basque cultural survival. There are, however, broader historic themes which have structured the evolution of each city within a local topography. Each has left a legacy in morphology, structures, and traditions which now provide the framework for city visiting and presentation (in

9

summary Sjoberg, 1965 and Claval, 1984; in detail Mumford, 1938 and Vance, 1977).

The earliest city function, *defence*, is evident from prehistoric hill forts to the formerly walled strip which now links east and west districts of Berlin. Fortified centres (such as Carcassone or Dubrovnik) now provide discrete visitor destinations, containment for an instant journey to a past where conflict is translated into colour and glamour. The development of defended places, often on hills, encouraged the consolidation of *local power*, both spiritual and temporal. Cities became seats, marked at their heart by upward reaching places of worship and fortified palaces which guarded the finance, arms, troops, supplies ... and centres of learning which underwrote continuing superiority. The legacy of this power is reflected in most of Europe's major urban destinations, from the cathedral in Stavanger in Norway, to the Arsenal in Venice, from the memorable skyline of Toledo, to a point of origin in the Acropolis of Athens. In many long-standing tourist venues, the cathedral within its characteristic town morphology, marks the focus of attention (Nairn and Browne, 1963). Pilgrimage was, of course, the first form of tourism.

The exercise of power for profit inevitably involved the development of local and regional trade. The city provided both physical *security* and restrictive *regulation* which ensured approved patterns of regional development, endorsed local product and craft specialisms, provided a regular market and a capacity for storage. Most significant, such a trading function endorsed the need for regulated public spaces in which such exchange took place. Central markets, fragmented through product specialism, and local community markets now provide the network of public spaces through which the visitor is drawn or herded; 'in underscoring the distinctiveness of the ensemble of European cities, it is the town square that must be emphasized' (Claval, 1984).

The successful development of local trade and its extension to distant markets often implied a major *entrepôt* base, with water transport, road improvement, and the warehouses, yards and residences for locals and foreigners associated with specific imports. This gave rise to dockyard and shipbuilding areas, to the earliest industrial zones, and to the emergence of specific 'quarters' identified with immigrant groups, crafts or products. Both the waterfronts and these quarters now provide discrete and marketable attractions, often at some remove from the city core.

Our image of the Western city remains dominated by the smokestacks and factories which mark the period from the late 18th to the late 20th century, that of *manufacturing*. Location in relation to raw materials and markets, together with the haphazard distribution of the entrepreneurs gave rise to a new pattern of towns and cities which both enveloped, and discarded, earlier sites. Those few traditional centres which were by passed may now have a particular cache as 'unspoilt', but few survived without some manufacture, and a scale of industrial building which generated a new morphology on the then urban edge. Traditions of craft and industry carried with them an integral local concern for design, later to be articulated in movements and revivals, such as those in Birmingham and Vienna at the turn of the 20th century. Much of the unacceptable face of the Western industrial city, its crowding and insanitary conditions, have been swept away, leaving a residue of converted mills and factories and rich, museum bound, collections of local artifacts (Watson, 1991).

Long before the rise of manufacturing, a form of *civic freedom* was fought for, and achieved, by the citizens of major cities, especially in the Low Countries. This emergence of the city governed by its citizens was marked by a prolonged phase of city making which sought to establish the primacy of local authority over religious or inherited power. The city hall and its various equivalents either rose over the neighbouring cathedral, or were set to dominate an established, or purpose-built, square. Public works and public buildings were designed for maximum impact, with newly adopted community functions, markets, schools, then parks, baths and transport systems, incorporating the credentials of the elected authority. In continuing public ownership, such features often retain their visual significance and function in the tourist town or city.

Beyond such displays of civic freedom and identity came the competition between manufacturing and trading centres. In advancing local cause and economy, the *displays of wealth*, such as music, painting and literature which were evident in earlier competition between royal, princely and churchly courts were re-interpreted by burghers, mayors and city officials in consort with monied benefactors. Such displays required a public, rather than private, setting for their impact and therefore generated *cultural patronage* on a grand scale which produced not only opera houses, concert halls, museums, galleries and celebratory spaces, but the orchestras, compositions, collections and events to occupy them; not only the cultural products on display, but the musical, artistic and craft training to ensure their continuance. These were often adjunct to established tourist destinations where historical associations had broadened religious pilgrimage (Brown and Fearon, 1939 and Gomme, 1964 on tourism in Stratford).

The late 19th century saw the rise of *city boosterism*, most evidently in North America, but easily identifiable in the city re-structuring, social and cultural provision which ushered in the beginning of a town planning profession (Gold & Ward, 1994). This period of inter-city competition, which provided the cultural and often the political, basis for nation building has continued unabated in some countries such as Germany and France. Others, such as Britain, have seen abrasive confrontation between central and city

11

power, most evident in the Prime Minister Thatcher's abolition of the Greater London Council and other English Metropolitan County Councils in the 1980s.

Phases in city growth and evolution have each left their most obvious mark in the physical structure of the city. Physical remnants have been endowed with meanings, reinforced and manipulated, to provide an acceptable urban heritage. The basic morphology, or plan structure of cities, closely tied to individual land ownership, is reinforced through time. In generations when buildings outlasted people, their survival was often ensured as essential to political and cultural continuity (see recent promotional volumes on Charleroi, Atelier Ledoux, 1993 and Leicester, 1993). It is this morphology of streets, places, watersides and views, and the accumulation of conserved structures - often at the city core - which provides the basis for modern tourism. To these may be added the heritage collections, from religious and princely acquisition, through civic collecting to private benefice. Such artifacts tend to fit within a narrow framework long established as 'Cultural' through the professional structures of commission and display - established creators creating for the establishment.

In the late 20th century there has been a realisation, first in the post Second World War era and now with the thirst for 'authentic' events, that supposedly 'popular' traditions also deserve retention. This has led to the collection and presentation of craft and popular arts which endorse popular culture and also the revival, relocation and reinvention of accessible events and 'homemade' products. There are few cities where supposedly authentic products of a craft industry which probably went underground in the 18th century cannot now be purchased, or where popular dances learned in high school, or at evening classes, are not paraded as key elements in local identity. Although there may be little continuity with the urban past, such events succeed in drawing visitors to underused spaces, and in animating architectural remains.

The visitor dips into an urban culture which is changing very rapidly. Participation in such change is usually more limited; major development sites are not on the tourist itinerary, immigrant quarters seldom the subject of guided tours, the new industrial estate or shopping centre (save where tax advantages apply) is not part of the heritage experience. Yet these contemporary changes are manufacturing a new heritage in their wake, and the heritage image to which so many cling, is itself being shaped in reaction to the commonplace change of a home city.

2.3 The city present

One reason why the heritage city is proving such a visitor attraction is that, in easily consumable form, it establishes assurance in a world which is changing rapidly. The contained morphology of an historic urban core re-establishes the city as a manifestation of order, community contribution and benevolent power (see Olsen's 1986 perspective). Watch faces on a cathedral visit to see individual reconciliation of current complexity with presumed historic confidence and simple order.

Modern urban life is marked strongly by the re-statement of our relationships with time and space. In most cases we have more, undesignated, time at our disposal with an inadequate structure to use it. The working day is generally shorter, as is the working week which, with a decline in the Christian Sunday, has become less structured. Annually there is more time devoted to vacations, and by living much longer, we accumulate substantial non-working time in later life. Add the obvious increase in mobility to these temporal changes, and at each scale - day, week, year, life - there is more flexibility to engage more places in the search for purpose or novelty. Only awareness, access, and wealth dictate the patterns which emerge. As a result, tourism has expanded and become the subject for extensive social comment (Turner & Ash, 1975; MacCannell, 1976; Hindley, 1983; Jakle, 1985; Urry, 1990; MacCannell, 1992).

The tentacles of public, and now private, transport have spread the concept of city into a network of overlapping and functioning regions (Whitehand, 1967). There is less need to live in, or indeed to go to, town than in the past. National maps, formerly peppered with towns and cities, are replaced by motorway maps which imply movement rather than fixity. We are encouraged to roam the system, drawn to nodes on the network in order to fulfil retail, service and leisure needs. At its fullest extent, this is the non-place city supposedly epitomised by Los Angeles (Muller, 1986; Johnson and Schaffer, 1994).

Personal transport has certainly encouraged residential flight. A key element of the historic city was the, often ill-provided, gathering of residences appropriate to each urban function in the immediate neighbourhood of a dominant structure. Since the late 19th century, public, then private transport spread the city to its region. In some cities, such as Paris or Prague, this leads to a schizophrenic life style with the car and motorway providing an essential link between the weekday apartment and the weekend rural retreat. In Britain the accessible, but pseudo-rural retreat, is the permanent home with the nearby city providing the workaday occasion for location. As working place, the central city survives only for working hours and whilst, in Southern Europe, the climatic response extends the working day into the evening, in Northern Europe and North America the 9 until 5 city centre has become the rule (Comedia, 1991). In the evening social energy circulates around the suburbs and the city centre is left to those who, through mobility or capital, are trapped there. Given the realisation that a living city needs residents, there has been a prolonged attempt to retain, and draw people back, to becalmed city centres. University quarters seem to succeed, but too often the newly established city centre residences are bastions against the alien culture without, as in the residential designs of London's Docklands.

A steady movement to the suburbs over the past century has meant that three or four generations may now broadly identify themselves with a city, without having any economic contact with its heart. They nevertheless identify the named city with their origins and supply, therefore, an important element of visitors to the city centre and its heritage assets. Their family and visitors expect to join in visits to the core and to establish, or re-establish, a relationship with a named place. Visiting the family in Izmir, Padua, Segovia or Oslo may mean driving to an edge suburb, but it may also mean a ritual trek through central sites and collections which are found to be occupied by those with a lesser claim to this, rapidy personalised, inheritance. Peripheral residents may expect a central legacy on the few occasions when they choose to use it, but their tangible investment is scarcely sufficient to ensure the survival of city centres. Focus of traffic movements and civic development in the past, the centres have suffered both from the damage which car traffic must bring, and the lack of local investment which has been diverted to peripheral locations.

Rumours as to the demise of the industrial city core were swept aside in the post Second World War reconstruction of many European cities; in North America the impact of suburban flight and spread city was clearer but unmet. From the 1940's to the 1960's many European cities carried on as if nothing was happening, rebuilding, tentatively adding to the central store of cultural monuments, and expecting vitality to follow. Bombed historical hearts, - as in Munster or Warsaw - were painstakingly reconstructed, not as tourist destinations, but as physical totems for the focusing of local and national culture. Elsewhere - as in Coventry and Rotterdam - the significance of the city centre was endorsed in modern (but essentially pre-war) style.

The relevance of traditional city centres was successively challenged by suburban residence and relocation, by new travel patterns, and especially by the re-structuring of urban industry. Production, office and service functions became 'footloose'. New peripheral re-development zones, such as London's Docklands, further sought to draw their strength from the established city centres. In the transition from industrial to post industrial city, manufacturing and its successors were, inevitably, seen as an essential element in place maintenance. New peripheral sites were increasingly liberated from rural or planning controls in order to retain attractive and accessible locations within the city's ambit. Thus peripheral business districts with associated suburban residential communities spread far beyond the city limits, extending to today's 'technopoles' (Garreau, 1991; Castells, 1989; Castells and Hall, 1994).

The process of city extension, and generation on the periphery left the centre in a parlous state, dominated largely by civic investment and residual communities and unable to take advantage of the new flexibility in residential and employment location. Belatedly centres have responded through the packaging of central city areas into districts or quarters which benefit from a morphology and built infrastructure, translated into a 'quarter' commodity, relying heavily on culture and the cultural industries. Universities, museums, performance places and relict public spaces have played an anchor role in the redevelopment of such areas and may become largely devoted to the tourist and visitor industries (Netzer, 1992; Yale, 1991).

The process of city planning that results from this major change is characterised by a managerial and investment-led approach to redevelopment (Smyth, 1994). Historic morphology and buildings provide the infrastructure for a process of small business revival, visitor attractions, and service industries which are expected to draw investment back to the city centre (as exemplified in Glasgow's regeneration, Keating, 1988; Boyle, 1991). Such 'quarters' have a mixed history, although they remain the current strategic choice in many European countries. They have a very clear relationship with the, sometimes nebulous, expectations of the tourist and visitor industries. Commodified character littered with conserved buildings is expected to draw visitors, who will then spend on galleries, museums, retail outlets and casual attractions. Some such zones have been able to report success (Law, 1992 & 1993). Their impact is to detach the favoured quarter from its surroundings and to incorporate locally alien elements. Travel patterns and media coverage have extended the city into its hinterland. The need for recognisable titles has meant that most peripheral communities are subsumed under the name of the nearest city, which itself has become a complex network of locally known places with a defined heritage location at the core.

At the close of the 20th Century our geography has been translated from one of located and experienced places to McLuhan's Global Village in which we are daily assaulted with a gazetteer of locations, only partially map supported, in which fundamental human actions shape reputation and potential. Media stereotypes painlessly construct our travel and vacation plans with road diversions re-directing daily journey-to-work patterns and international events inviting or repelling our advances (Zonn, 1990). Three Tenors cap the World Cup Football Final in Los Angeles, the stars attend, and all memories of urban conflict are forgiven. Refugees flee from Rwanda into other parts of Africa, and all Africa as a visitor destination is blighted. Little wonder that extremists now focus their bombing attention on tourists in Turkey, or unsettle the emerging image of Spain's Basque country.

Travel range is, of course, conditioned by personal finances. Many only manage a day out at the seaside, or less. But the mobile population is sufficient, growing and rich, to allow new tourist venues to emerge, and for their novelty to be a major attraction. The media purveyed 'liberation' of eastern and central Europe was quickly mobilised into a sequence of new venues. As major cities such as Prague and Budapest show clear signs of overcrowding, so a secondary series of 'undiscovered' towns is currently being marketed to a western population.

Novelty is a key commodity in the marketing of tourist and visitor venues, and the superficiality of televised images ensures that the most packageable of buildings and events reach the television screen as appropriate vacation investments. Coupled with media promotion, the search for novelty tends to consume historic town centres, skimming only the most evident and packaged elements of urban form and experience. City regeneration has tended to pander to this market, leading to the capacity problems which are the focus here. The continual search for novelty by the travel industry can lead to the rapid disposal of discarded centres. For many cities, visitor spending may only provide a temporary solution to the more fundamental problems of central area regeneration, and coping with future patterns of urban living.

2.4 The city future

Many European countries have rejected the inevitability of North American development patterns, but the effectiveness of a planning process in containing and retaining the historic city has been severely questioned, both in legislative change, and in practice over the past decade. The demand for peripheral space and economic survival has overruled development constraints in many increasingly free market oriented economies, with employment prospects and economics perceived as more fundamental to national wellbeing than the trappings of past cultures.

Stimulated by North America's economic outlook, and possibly by its inward looking political perspective, trans-Atlantic models are now being widely adopted throughout the world. Most notable are the transnational linkages between cities and regions, re-defining the world map into trading and communication associations which span the world. The sheer magnitude of such linkages is sufficient to cause many to seek the comfort of the historic city. The Pacific Rim is, perhaps, the clearest example of such linkages, drawing North America from Europe to a concentration on south Asia, and Australasia. In South America, too, associations between Brazil and Argentina in the south, and between Mexico and its northern neighbours promise to be the relationships which matter in the next century.

Numerous transnational lines of linkage have been defined for Europe and most are liable to modification, around the established patterns which connect

London with Rotterdam, with Paris and Frankfurt (see Dunford & Perrons, 1994). Accepting their peripheral status to this established link, the Mediterranean port cities of Spain, France and Italy have gone further than most in referring to their mutual interests. Such new patterns are intended to aid the survival of involved cities, and will also internationalise their infrastructure. As such, it is all the more important to re-state the local significance from which such developments are built (Le Goff and Guieysse, 1985).

Barcelona, the exemplar international city, has pursued a decade long programme to reinforce its community, tourist, and Catalan significance as a basis for its role as a major international centre (Goodey, 1994a). The successful Olympic presentation was a vehicle by which physical changes and media images could be effected at a range of scales. Barcelona has been quite clear in its purpose of playing in the highest international leagues. The casual 'Europe's Best Cities' lists which bemuse the flight magazine reader represent the surface of a very competitive series of races indulged in by a wide range of European cities (Goodey, 1992). Environmental quality, social infrastructure, labour relations and connectivity are the major variables which business locators consider when fixing their international offices. These are the key elements in making, or breaking, cities in the international race. Whilst hardly an afterthought, heritage and culture are useful additions, rather than essential ingredients, to success. Culture is, however, far more imageable than, for example, a successful secondary school or hospital emergency department. Hence cultural attractions feature in promotional brochures and campaigns. A new museum, collection, orchestral conductor, or building by a star architect is an accessible, physical manifestation of a lively and capital attracting economy. City 'star quality' is discussed across occupational and role lines, so the city which attracts a Fair (Ley and Olds, 1988), a Garden Festival, a cultural attribution, or sporting event is likely to be rewarded both by business investment and by tourist visitors who will, however, seek very different things from their association. Implications for the full range of city residents are explored by Loftman, Middleton and Nevin (1994).

Present patterns of mobility and attachment suggest the continued evolution of the dual purpose city; a safe, secure and, increasingly, arcadian home to the majority (though not all) of the residents, and an exciting, packaged, heritage experience for the visitor. The two populations meet at times of central celebration, or if one strays into the territory of the other, but the overlap may be limited. Visitors are seldom invited to extend their exploration to residential or peripheral industrial areas, residents select peripheral retail and service opportunities so as to avoid the pressure of visitors at the centre.

Extrapolating from the present we can envisage the proliferation and maturing of edge city places where, as in North America, mall or retail based communities quickly develop their own culture and heritage although experts on the city still find difficulty in adjusting to new forms (but see Bishop's 1986 research report on Milton Keynes in this regard). Increasingly, the centre may be perceived as a venue, with specialist retailing and an impressive array of events and exhibitions. Competition between centres stimulates novelty and the 'fun', or 'themed', nature of urban centres overlaps with the overtly commercial themed attractions (illustrated in futuristic proposals for the redevelopment of Croydon, see Goodey 1993). The 'fun' city meets the theme park but with the added ingredient of 'real' history.

Consequences, such as the total collapse of centres unable to keep up with the media stimulated race, can be envisaged. But more significant is the all-pervading sense that the individual mobility provided by the car cannot much longer be tolerated. Within the decade intolerable mobility, and the geography that it has created, is likely to be curtailed by a combination of environmental health issues, fuel economics and a re-statement of public morality. Whilst 'sustainability' as an operational tag has been over used and misunderstood, the pressures for city management and planning which reflect more closely changing individual recognition of present unsustainability are likely to have a major impact on future development patterns. The more sustainable form of the traditional city core will be re-discovered, public transport will be re-invigorated, and individual investment in journeys will decrease. Hopefully, the management of access to, and marketing, of heritage and natural attractions will undergo a fundamental reappraisal.

2.5 City identity

A key element in attracting and sustaining visitors, as well as validating the residential decision of those who call it home, is the identity, or image of a city (Ashworth and Voogd, 1990; Ashworth and Goodall, 1990; Keith and Pile, 1993; Kearns and Philo, 1993). But, although contemporary marketing may suggest otherwise, no city has a single identity or image. The past will have provided a rich array of structures, events, associations and characters upon which to build, whilst the particular interests which visitor or resident brings to the place will shape the daily search, and the communicated message. Personal experiences, reported crimes, sports successes and the birthplaces of personalities are amongst the unmanaged elements which can shape or redirect a city's image.

In discussing heritage city centres, we must recognise the very long traditions which many cities have in image development (Ousby, 1990). We could teach the 18th century promoters of a city such as Bath little in the way of destination management (Corfield, 1982). The built form was designed so as to establish a strong visual image, events were promoted and presented so as to heighten each participant's experience and ensure a positive report in the press, and for more prolonged effect in the popular novels of the day. The local press was drawn into a central role in the city's promotion, and royalty and politicians were favoured so that positive images filtered through to seats of power. Bath's cultural development as a resort destination was inextricably linked to the development of speculative housing and of public buildings.

Contemporary promotion and marketing have, however, served to simplify these historic methods. Although urban promotion shows continuity since Bath's rise (Burgess, 1982), with the selling of model industrial communities, garden cities and trading estates, it has now become associated with rather different company. Whilst many cities retain staff for the promotion of business and industrial opportunities, selling the city image is often diverted to another agency. City image advocacy has become linked to tourist and cultural marketing and focuses on the establishment of a 'unique selling proposition' in the media users mind. In this process, where short, concise, media images are essential, the visual attributes of a city are synthesised to a sequence of colour-/and sound-full impressions which compete with the current array of similar promotions (Jarvis, 1987). Such images are tuned to a presumed, and sometimes researched, estimate of market interest, with an emphasis on those likely to spend most money, if not time, in an historic city core. Inevitably there is a sameness in the marketing of historic city centres - the medieval spire, the guard or musician in costume, a horse-drawn vehicle, a spread of the local dishes, a willow-draped waterside and the rest.

In turn, these market images then have an impact on the way in which visitors meet the city, with spaces, places and events revised or invented so as to extend the range of opportunities within the acceptable framework. The local planning strategies may be shaped to meet visitors' expectations of the chershished image (Daniels, 1992 account of England's Constable country). New sculpture, and cultural structures, find a special place in such promotional campaigns, as evidence of a city's interest in supporting public art and sharing the fame which, in many cultures, accrues to the successful architect. This does not work in all cultures, but in Spain, France, Italy and Germany the association with a fashionable designer is as important as the eventual function of the structure. In Birmingham a provocative period of public art investment was, however, subsequently rebutted (Cohen, 1993).

Whilst city promotion can never afford to become entirely two-faced, there is every danger that the image endorsed through local conversation, a lively local press, local political debate, and individual life experiences will be at variance with that promoted by city authorities. City centre promotional literature and national press coverage may highlight a world apart from city residents. Such a separation of images can have a significant impact on

19

relationships between residents and visitors and tends to reinforce a locally perceived image of a tourist zone no-go area. With the reduction of historic city assets to increasingly terse phrases and images - such as the 'I Love' heart motif - there is also the tendency to remove the controversial, incorrect or inelegant. In terms of heritage and visitor attractions, there has been a noticeable reduction in the number of zoo and animal images in promotional literature in recent years, whilst some building types such as prisons, hospitals and working class housing, however significant, do not feature. Similar observations might be made of the young, the old, the disabled, the poor and the immigrant populations who form an essential part of our city centres.

2.6 The heritage resource

With its increasingly frequent use over the past twenty years, the term 'heritage' has become extended, some might say over extended, in meaning (NRIT, 1983; Hobsbawm and Ranger, 1983; Wright, 1985; Hewison, 1987; Corner and Harvey, 1991; Clark et al, 1994; Goodey, 1994b). In English, where it has latterly become an acceptable governmental cipher for involvement in 'culture' through the Department of National Heritage, the term has strong links with the idea of a national 'inheritance'. This implies a passing on of nationally recognised items of value from one generation to the next, with the assumption that these will be held in trust for successive generations. In Britain, the list of elements recognised as heritage has only recently been extended from the tradition of buildings and fine art, to include nature, landscapes, engineering, industrial remains and the recorded oral tradition (Delevoy, 1975; Goodall, 1993). It is important to recognise, however, that the valued heritage of other cultures, whilst almost always including buildings and fine art, may place more emphasis on literary and musical cultures, and on the landscapes which are said to have stimulated them. Cultural and period differences in heritage identification are relentlessly explored in Lowenthal and Binney (1981) and in Lowenthal's (1985) study of nostalgia.

Public definitions of heritage are still largely dominated by highly educated professionals with expertise in fine art, architecture, engineering, literature, music or design whose professional future is underpinned by generating an academic, problem-based, literature on their subject. This often places the professional at considerable remove from the visitor's need for succinct and graphic information although museums have, inevitably, responded to market needs (Lumley, 1988; Vergo 1989; Walsh, 1992; Johnson and Thomas, 1992; Myerson, 1994). The emerging profession of interpretation has developed to bridge this long standing gap, but fine art and architectural history

20

professionals remain the only respected advisers in heritage management in many countries. Their role in maintaining buildings and architectural detail as central to heritage definition deserves reappraisal.

Although surviving buildings have meaning to the visitor, it is seldom the meaning with which they are endowed by the professional. Much more interesting than a minor step forward in building technology, or decorative device are often the human associations and events which surround a structure - 'the room where', 'the balcony from which' etc. This serves to underline the fact that the most common elements in a heritage require little conservation, for they are the images, memories and oral traditions which are passed, with modification, to the next generation and to new arrivals in a community. This is a dynamic heritage where unnecessary elements are discarded and new elements (such as pop music associations) are added. Significant, too, in a personal heritage are associations with events or characters which achieve national or international recognition. The subject is complex but the fact that many more people can identify what they were doing when they heard that President Kennedy had been assassinated, than can remember their circumstances when 'Man first set foot on the Moon' is significant. Sensation, tragedy and crime sustain the 'normal' imagination and seek reference in a popular heritage.

Surviving buildings, on the other hand, tend to express power or authority to the majority of viewers. The conserved school, courthouse, railway station or factory may well stimulate positive ... or negative ... memories and thus serve as catalyst to a more personal heritage. Interestingly, the basic morphological layout of city streets, blocks, ownerships and accessways, though fundamental to the subsequent city image and location of heritage in context has only latterly been recognised both as a guide to contemporary city reconstruction, and as a significant source for resident and visitor comprehension.

Such comprehension is essential if heritage is not to be the passing of the past to the future without any intervening involvement by the current generation. The tradition of marvel and wonderment at seeing a structure, view, or artefact for the first time has been largely removed by the all-invasive eyes of photography and television. Walking and experiencing in context may be sufficient, but there is often a desire for 'hands on' experience, regardless as to whether the heritage element can withstand such continual blessing. Those who have seen Byron's name carved on ancient Greek stone, or the legacy of such inscriptions in many cathedrals, will recognise continuity here, but it is the sheer numbers of those seeking involvement that have their impact on heritage remains. Even with the commonplace of local parish churches, the desire to explore comes up against the necessity to secure (Somerville, 1994); volume and access bring both searchers and destroyers.

National and local responses to heritage, and to its various constituents, range along a continuum from *preservation* through *conservation*, to *presentation, interpretation, commodification* and even *replication*. The first decision is whether to preserve, in what context and in what form. The revived folk ballad may be translated to a contemporary language to aid understanding, whilst the industrial winding gear may be checked, re-painted and left as a landmark. More often, conservation is essential in order to ensure that the structure, artefact or ephemeral creation are retained for future generations. Inevitably the conservation process, itself, will involve modification of the item, applying the values and techniques of the current generation. The well intentioned sequence of measures applied to the Acropolis through time provides an interesting lesson in changing conservation attitudes, with current conservators ensuring that nothing which they do cannot be undone in the light of future technology and values.

In the second half of the 20th century there has been a phenomenal increase in the range of heritage designations and the increasing realisation that this very public form of collecting cannot be justified without access for the public. Although the battle is still joined in museum circles the clear implication has emerged that if public money is to be used to defend heritage, then the public should be able to benefit from and enjoy the legacy without damaging it, and quite probably the public should also pay for the pleasure. At the very least this argument implies that heritage should be made accessible through presentation, and that probably a mediating body of interpretation is required in order to enhance the visitor's experience. Such interpretation, which may involve not only text and sound, but events and actors in 'first person presentation', walks the line between presentation and commodification of heritage. A strong case can be, and has been, made for such commodified 'experiences' where replication, reconstruction or idealisation of an historic structure, item or event provides the focus for a well managed visitor destination, whilst protecting the original heritage. More questionable are the entertainments which claim a spurious authenticity and have little or no link with their context (Prentice, 1993). In criticism, Walsh (1992, 149) reflects a frequent view:

> One important characteristic of post modern heritage has been its unnerving ability to deny historical process, or diachrony. Heritage successfully mediates all our pasts as ephemeral snapshots exploited in the present, to embellish decaying cityscapes, and to guarantee the success of capital in its attempt to develop new superfluous markets.

In transforming heritage from an educated and professional enthusiasm to a broader appeal, the term 'popularise' is used in some cultures, whilst 'democratise' finds favour in other parts of Europe. It is the tension between these two terms that holds the key to effective transformation and management of heritage and its visitors. Popularisation carries with it implications of debasement, or simplification, of theme park fun and a lack of reverence; it certainly implies the sharing of a private, conservators', world with a broad body of more casual observers. Democratisation, in a cultural sense, gives purpose and responsibility to this process. A national or city heritage is the inheritance of all. In the past we have, unknowingly, dedicated professional skills to the past, but there is no reason why the allocation of funds, and indeed the values to be embodied in conservation, should not enjoy a broader public remit. Single issue local tax votes in the United States, and the common employment of subscriber trusts and foundations for heritage elsewhere, begin to make this broader responsibility a reality. Britain's choice of a national lottery to support heritage investment is another, less obvious, path to the same end.

The importance of popularisation/democratisation is particularly important at the local, city level. Here residents live daily with both their heritage and the visitors to it. For local identity to survive, it must be regularly reinvigorated by community contributions. The link between a local heritage and today's population must be a living link, expressed through use, as well as by financial support. In identifying and designing revised or new heritage 'experiences' the local population upon whom such proposals will impact must be considered, not only because of the physical inconveniences which may result in the short or long term, but because it is _their_ local identity which is being manipulated. The case study of Oxford below is significant in this regard, as it is a city which has endured a lengthy historical conflict with incomers, be they students or tourists.

2.7 Manifest culture and the cultural industries

The same informed professional guardianship which has invested building with such heritage meaning is applied to a range of art forms which have been designated for enduring public funding and are identified as 'high culture', as the core of the performing arts. Here too, we must be careful not to presume that attitudes prevailing in one culture are appropriate to all, or that styles of presentation and clientele are fixed for all time. Symphony orchestra performances are instructive. In Britain these have been locked, until recently, in forbidding concert halls where ticket price, programmes, costume and critical appraisal have all endorsed an art apart from the majority of the population. Suddenly Britain has discovered the alfresco evening concert, suddenly the British weather (or our attitude towards it) has changed, suddenly

Walkman and CD sized themes are fit for playing, and the park context is readily available. Television has played a positive role in making performances, and gallery collections, more accessible to a wider public in those countries where traditions of patronage and attendance did not already draw on a broad community. Whilst media presentation may have reinforced established and staid elements in the repertoire, it has also provided the finance for more experiment than would otherwise be available. The potential for worldwide networked, video or CD audiences has also upgraded the status, and probably the quality, of less established cultural forms and performers.

The emergence of the term 'cultural industries' to include both high and emerging cultural forms, and to link creators, with performers, with venues, with those who reproduce and distribute performances has served to both democratise and validate the economic contribution which such activities make to urban life. However, in doing so there has been an inevitable reduction in the, albeit elitist, mystique surrounding the creativity which is at its core (the pioneer report here is by Myerscough, 1988 see also Bianchini, Fisher and Worple, 1991; Arts Council of Great Britain, 1989).

Together with the more recent emergence of public art (Flemming and von Tscharner, 1987; Roberts, Marsh and Salter, 1993) and the revitalisation of city landscape design (Magnus, 1992), the established traditions of theatre, musical performance, opera, ballet and dance, and art gallery presentation represent the living heritage of any city. In the leagues of city competition they are regarded as priority assets, unquestioned in their significance to a rich and creative urban environment. They provide the occasion for most new public buildings, and the most accessible path to widespread television and video coverage. As the numerous conflicts between world class conductors and their city authorities have shown, some branches of the cultural industry are major players on the international urban heritage scene. Cities are encouraged to respond to creative genius through the allocation of appropriate settings, both enclosed and open air, which provide a context for performance or imageable art. Such spaces and events become a key element in the visitor itinerary, especially if combined with an international conference venue, which is presumed to draw the paying international audience for some featured cultural events (Van Beetz et al, 1989; Getz, 1991; Hall, 1992). The developing concept of 'cultural planning' can mean much more (Montgomery, 1990; Griffiths, 1993; Lim, 1993) although its implications are resisted in some European countries.

But there is another side to the development of urban cultural industries, far distant from the jetting lead tenor or gallery opening. Cultural innovation has long been born of the anonymity and protection which the city provides. Rare, marginal, people have been able to find kindred souls with whom to develop ideas in cheap surroundings. The city has offered space, stimulus, and a market

24

place for such innovation, be it in literature, art, music or design. Today such creativity has been harnessed by urban authorities who see their restored heritage quarters as providing an appropriate setting for such activity, with obvious spin-offs for local services and skills. Not a few quarter regeneration plans place the cultural industries at the centre of their proposals, but with the clear implication that a somewhat bohemian area will also provide a visitor attraction. It is too early to evaluate any benefits which may accrue to either the city, or the cultural industries in this replication of a previously productive context, although the presumed significance of the recording industry, surely as footloose as any, gives cause for concern (Cohen, 1991). More certain are the benefits to both performers and visitors of the increase in street artists in our cities. The worldwide context of managed performance spaces which require animation has generated a novel range of skilled artists, now often auditioned by the managing authority, but providing a point of access to dance, theatre and circus without detracting from their surroundings.

The notion of cultural 'industries' has been an effective promotional tool for the arts, and for cities which can see few opportunities in their traditional industries (see Bianchini, 1990; Bianchini, Dawson and Evans, 1990; Barnett, 1991; Bianchini and Parkinson, 1993). Although excessive economic claims have seemed to be the rule, rather than the exception, in proposal brochures, the extended cultural industries are here to stay. Whether they incorporate 'the heritage industry' and therefore bridge the divide between creativity and conservation is a moot point. In the study which follows we conceive of urban heritage and cultural opportunities as offering one, promoted and managed market, to the city visitor.

2.8   Managing the future

Heritage, the cultural industries, and the images of cities and towns are drawn into a new association to be marketed as a major, in places *the* major asset. The product is one of images and flows, of superficial sharing:

> One of the Randstad's strong points is the recurring allusion to architectural, economic and civic traditions on a smaller scale, in Dutch towns such as Alkmaar, Leyden, Haarlem, Delft, Dordrecht, Gouda and Utrecht. It is an image which confirms the significance of the towns for the culture of the Randstad. (Van Beetz, 1989)

The study which follows examines an issue which has become significant to both local populations and visitors in a world wide range of urban (and rural) locations. On the one hand, there are visitors spontaneously seeking to share the experience of a prized local asset, visitors encouraged to come to a city in order to underpin a failing economic structure, visitors drawn to see a contemporary creation of quality. On the other hand, local residents either secure in their pace of change, or jolted by misfortune or opportunity, find their places and spaces dominated by those with different behaviour, language, financial circumstances and agendas. The city is modified through parking regulation, building access, service provision, crowding and damage which must, it seems, result from this influx of visitors. (De Bres, 1994). Change, which is inevitable in the nature of a city, is blamed on the visitor, communities are not consulted, and are drawn ever inward and apart from their city cores. Suburban residents range free in a lifestyle which is increasingly unsustainable.

The heritage assets of any city can be consumed. The single, uninspiring, visit represents not-to-be repeated consumption for resident and visitor alike. Overuse and poor management can lead to the deterioration of the physical asset, and to a decline also in community goodwill which is reflected in service performance and ambience. Dominance of a market economy over creativity in the arts can easily lead to repeated, increasingly sterile, performances. By engaging the heritage and cultural industries in the mainstream of urban survival we have, on balance, drawn them closer to both the local and the visiting communities. But neither represents an endless resource. In some cities the process of exploitation has developed so rapidly that already significant impacts on the quality of community and cultural life are evident. Elsewhere, the process has hardly begun. By considering good practice within the framework of the carrying capacity concept, this study seeks to inform and alert city managers and the tourist industries to the dangers, and the opportunities, which appear in the immediate future.

3 Tourism impacts

3.1 Introduction

Although it is difficult to accurately quantify, tourism is, arguably, the world's largest industry, accounting for about 5½ percent of the world's GNP and 6 per cent of employment, and it is growing fast. International tourism is estimated to have increased from 25 million in 1950 to 429 million in 1990 (WTO, 1993); and predictions suggest an increase to over 600 million by the year 2000. Most countries encourage tourism. For poor countries, regions, towns and cities it is seen as the fast track to development. For historic towns and cities, the 'commodification' of heritage and culture for tourist consumption may be seen as bringing many economic benefits for little investment. But at what cost? The Hague Declaration on Tourism (1989) referred to a 'tourism revolution', with real and potential impacts on people, economies and the environment. As with most revolutions, there is a price to pay, and a number of story leaders in the British popular press such as *Death by Tourism* (Nicholson-Lord, 1990), *The Enchanted Nightmare* (Hamilton, 1990) and *Sights for Sore Eyes* (Vulliamy, 1992) serve well to illustrate the costs associated with some recent growth in the industry.

Tourism contains the seeds of its own destruction; tourism can kill tourism destroying the very environmental attractions which visitors come to a location to experience (Plog, 1974). There is a growing concern about tourism impacts and approaches to their effective management. This chapter provides a brief overview of the growth of interest in tourism impacts, the analysis of such impacts, and the role of processes and procedures such as environmental impact assessment (EIA).

27

3.2 Increasing concern about tourism impacts: a suitable case for treatment

Tourism can bring many economic benefits to a historic centre - most important it can bring jobs. Early analysis of tourism impacts focused on such benefits. But even the economic impacts have limitations, and there are also social and physical environmental impacts. For Butler (1980), capacity thresholds occur when the number of tourists approaches levels which strain the capability of the host area to provide a good visitor experience (Figure 3.1). The response to such thresholds can range from rejuvenation through to decline, and often with a change in the type of visitor. Doxey's 'irridex' (irritation index - Figure 3.2) charted one possible pathway of local social response to increasing visitor numbers - from euphoria to xenophobia (Doxey, 1975). The physical impacts can be the erosion and destruction of the valued natural and built environment. If we are to avoid Krippendorf's 'happy apocalypse' (Krippendorf, 1993), the analysis and management of tourism impacts needs to be at the top of the agenda for research and action in tourism. There are some positive signs, including a growing interest in the sustainability of tourism, the development of associated assessment processes such as EIA and approaches to visitor management, but the level of concern does vary between the participants in the tourism development process.

Tourism impacts result from the interaction between tourists, with their associated developments, and the host environments. Both parties to this interaction, and transaction, are multi-dimensional in character. Visitors to historic towns and cities vary in many ways and with resultant different impacts. There are day and overnight visitors, visitors of different nationalities, age, gender and income, and with different levels of awareness, understanding and expectations of the visited location. They may come to a location in several ways, independently or on a stage of a 'package tour', individually or 'en masse'. There are various well documented typologies of visitor types: for example - drifter, explorer, individual mass tourist, organised mass tourist (Cohen, 1978). Visitors also generate many associated goods and services, often known as the components of the tourism industry. These include tour operators, providers of accommodation and transport, restaurants, specialist retailers, manufacturers, specialist attractions and interpretation facilities additional to the existing heritage attraction.

The host environment is also multi-dimensional. A narrow definition of the environment would focus primarily on the natural (biophysical) and built environment. But this is too narrow, and tourism does tend to be one of the more enlightened areas in taking a more holistic approach to the environment, including also the vitally important social and economic dimensions. The social interaction between 'visitors' and 'hosts' is an important ingredient in the

Figure 3.1   Butler's model of the hypothetical evolution of a tourist area

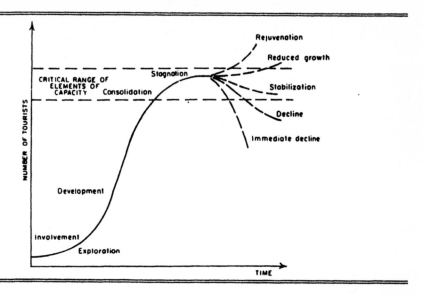

Source: Butler, 1980

Figure 3.2   Doxey's 'irridex' (irritation index)

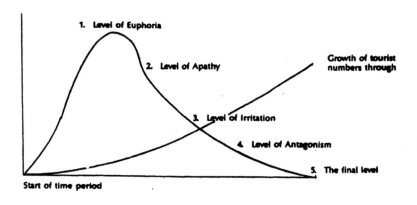

Source: Doxey, 1975

tourist experience. Economic impacts are a prime motivator for many of the participants in the transaction/ interaction. Historic towns and cities vary also in scale, from small, often single attraction centres such as Lourdes and Delphi, to major cities such as Paris and Athens. Historic centres vary also in their stage of development, including tourism development, and in their planning and management systems. As with tourists and associated developments, host environments are also dynamic, and undergoing change, irrespective of tourism.

Recent British government publications have emphasized the importance of maintaining the balance in tourism - between visitors and the host environment, between development and conservation (ETB, 1991). There is also an emerging interest in sustainable tourism development. The seminal 'Brundtland' Report defines sustainable development as that 'which meets the needs of the present generation without compromising the ability of future generations to meet their own needs' (UN, 1987). Sustainable development involves the maintenance, and hopefully enhancement, of various 'capital stocks' for future generations. In the context of historic towns and cities, this means not only 'man-made capital' such as historic buildings, but also 'human capital' such as local traditions, skills and customs, and 'natural/environmental' capital, such as clean air, fresh water and diversity of flora and fauna. There is however, a danger of 'sustainable development' becoming a weak catch-all phrase and there are already many alternative definitions, Turner and Pearce (1992) and Pearce (1992) have drawn attention to alternative interpretations of maintaining the capital stock. A 'weak sustainability' position could involve maintenance of the total capital stock, whilst running down one part of it, as long as there is substitutability between capital degradation in one area and investment in another. Such an approach is dangerous for historic centres, where replacement or substitution of lost capital may be difficult and where visitors are sensitive to environmental losses. A stronger sustainability position may be needed to maintain the valued environments of historic centres.

A useful summary of the key principles of sustainable tourism development, drawing on studies by the English and Welsh Tourist Boards and others, is provided by Elwyn Owen et al (1993):

. tourism is a potent economic activity which brings tangible benefits to the host community as well as to the visitor; however tourism is not a panacea and must form part of a balanced economy;

. the physical and cultural environments have intrinsic values which outweigh their values as tourism assets; their enjoyment by future generations and long term survival should not be prejudiced by short term considerations;

. the scale and pace of tourism development should respect the character of the area. Value for money and a high quality tourist experience should be promoted;

- the goal of optimum long term economic benefit to the community as a whole should be pursued, rather than short term speculative gain for only a few; and
- tourism development should be sensitive to the needs and aspirations of the host population. It should provide for local participation in decision making and the employment of local people.

The achievement of sustainable tourism development requires 'working partnerships among the network of actors and linking scientific research and public consultation to decision making' (Globe, 1990). The network of actors involves tourism developers and operators who produce the components of heritage tourism; tourists and locals who consume the experience and the visitor impacts in various forms; regulators, often government bodies, from international to local levels, plus various 'facilitators', including consultants, advisors and advocates. The awareness of UK regulators has already been noted through the 'Tourism and Environment' guidance initiatives of the early 1990s (ETB, 1991, 1993). Planning Policy Guidance, in the form of PPG21 (DoE, 1992) is also trying to nudge the planning of tourism in a sustainable direction. At the European Union Level, the Fifth Community Action Programme on the Environment, 'Towards Sustainability' (CEC, 1992) identifies tourism as one of the key sectors for action. EU environmental policy seeks the 'precautionary principle' approach, with a focus on preventative action, rectification of environmental damage at source, and payment by the polluters. The Fifth Programme advocates a mix of instruments including legislative and market based, supported by improved data, and spatial and sectoral planning. 'Agenda 21', the action plan from the UN Conference on Environment and Development held in Rio (UN, 1992) also draws attention to the impacts of tourism.

The tourism industry is also taking initiatives. Middleton and Hawkins (1994) comment that:

1990-92 was a watershed period for larger commercial organisations in travel and tourism, a period marking a shift in attitudes to the environment from a perception of it as a free resource to a recognition that the quality of the environment and the principles of sustainability have to be absorbed in corporate policy and programmes.

The World Travel and Tourism Council (WTTC), representing over sixty of the world's major tourism operators, has launched an Environment and Development initiative. This includes a focus on self-regulation by the industry, and the spread of good practice, based on research. Some of the latter is carried out by the World Travel and Tourism Environment Research Centre

(WTTERC) at Oxford Brookes University in the UK. The core of WTTERC's work is the collection, analysis and dissemination of information on the travel and tourism industry's response to growing international awareness of environmental problems. A number of key databases have been constructed on: examples of good environmental practice in the travel and tourism industry; company environmental policies; national and international regulations particularly relevant to tourism and the environment; and sources, for example on how to carry out an environmental audit or environmental impact assessment. In 1994, WTTC also introduced its 'Green Globe' initiative. This seeks to encourage the self-regulation by companies through the regular monitoring of, and reporting on, environ-mental performance. Guidance on improvement in performance is provided through WTTERC topic and sector specific documents, and via the resources of the WTTERC's databases.

Middleton and Hawkins (1994) summarise the leading company responses to environmental issues as comprising:

. more efficient use of energy;
. control of emissions of noise and atmospheric polluting chemicals;
. control of waste generated in traditional operating practices;
. more efficient use of fresh water;
. control of pollution arising from the use and disposal of hazardous materials used in operations;
. treatment and control of pollution arising from disposal of waste water and sewage;
. reduction/avoidance of damage caused to flora and fauna; and
. control over environmental impact through purchasing policies and contracting (inputs used in the conduct of business operations).

Martin Brackenbury, president of the International Federation of Tour Operators (IFTO), noted the major change amongst large tourism operators in his comments in the WTTERC's Environment and Development Newsletter (1993):

> Environmental considerations are shaping our business now. Our principal destinations in Europe are among the most threatened by the growth of tourism. It is inevitable that anyone supplying holidays is going to have their activities scrutinised for their compatibility with the ethic of sustainable tourism.

This view may not yet have percolated down to the hundreds of thousands of small businesses involved in tourism, and this constitutes a major problem for sustainable development in tourism. In addition, what of the other actors in the tourism development process - do the visitors and hosts care? Our studies suggests that the travelling public and the local populations of historic centres are becoming increasingly aware of, and sensitive to, the quality of environment, but there are many variations in the personal 'trade-offs' between the costs and benefits involved.

Both the diagnosis of problems and the prescription of policy measures have been aided in recent years by the development of planning and management tools. These include EIA, approaches to carrying capacity, and a variety of management methods.

3.3 Tourism impacts: the economic, socio-cultural and physical dimensions

The traditional approach to tourism impacts, well documented by authors such as Mathieson and Wall (1982) and Pearce (1989), focuses on the economic, social and physical environmental impacts of tourism. Research into tourism impacts initially centred on the economic impacts as these were more quantifiable and often positive. More recently there has been a shift towards consideration of the physical and social impacts. These are often typified as unquantifiable and negative - the ecological and social price for the economic benefit. Visitor management involves a trade off between these impacts. The equation may be shifting from how much ecology and local society can the economy stand to how much economy can the ecology and local society stand.

Economic impacts

Much analysis of economic impacts focuses on national and regional level benefits (Williams and Shaw, 1988; de Kadt, 1979). Tourism can be the catalyst for national and regional development, bringing employment, exchange earnings, balance of payments advantages and important infrastructure developments benefitting locals and visitors alike. This scenario has recently been very apt for the emerging democracies of eastern and central Europe, and their historic towns and cities have a key role to play. Yet such economic benefits can be considerably overstated. Poorly developed economies may not be able to meet tourist demands without major imports of goods and services; benefits can leak - and the financial flows can be likened to the flow from a tap into a bath without a plug (Glasson, 1992). The tourism multiplier, in its many forms, is an attempt to measure such leakages (Archer, 1977, 1982). Historic towns and cities may have a particular problem here in that much of the environment (physical and socio-cultural) may be a 'free good', generating little financial benefit for residents.

33

At the local level, the distribution of economic benefits will vary according to the ability of the local economy to provide visitor services, and according to the nature of the visitors. A city with a well developed tourist infrastructure (including locally owned accommodation, restaurant, retailing and entertainment components) and a range of attractions, may gain substantial per visitor economic benefit, particularly from staying/overnight visitors. In contrast some historic centres, either by virtue of limited infrastructure and/or location en route between other centres, may have short stay day visitors, with externally based travel operators being the main beneficiaries. The estimation of the extent of local benefits is best informed through questionnaire surveys of local visitors which can provide detailed pictures of the total, and mix of, visitor expenditure. This constitutes the 'multiplicand', the initial injection for the multiplier analysis. The multiplier provides a measure of how much of the initial injection of income stays in the local economy, and may be of the order of 0.2 to 0.3, for the (unorthodox) income multiplier (Pearce, 1989).

In addition to the leakage of benefits, there may be other costs. The seasonality of employment is often regarded as a devaluation of the employment benefit, although this may be less of a problem for built heritage attractions than for those more dependent on the weather. Other economic costs may include inflation in local markets, such as accommodation and restaurants, the 'crowding out' of local shops and services by those demanded by tourists, and over dependence on what can be a fickle industry susceptible to variables such as politics, crime and rumour.

Socio-cultural impacts

These are typified as the 'people impacts' of tourism with a focus on the impacts on the host community. They normally include both social impacts, concerned with the changes in the day-to-day quality of life of residents in tourist destinations, and cultural impacts, concerned with changes in traditional ideas and values, norms and identities resulting from tourism. Social and cultural impacts are strongly interrelated. As with physical and economic impacts, socio-cultural impacts are not limited only to the host area population; they are significant for the visitors themselves and for transit areas to visitor destinations. The interesting and significant issue of 'endearment' of tourists to destinations is only beginning to be understood, as research effort becomes directed to the impacts on tourists, in addition to the impacts on their hosts (see Prentice *et al*, 1994).

The socio-cultural impacts result from the interaction between 'hosts' and 'guests' (Smith, 1989). A number of factors may contribute to difficulties in this relationship. The transitory nature of a visit to a historic centre may be too short to allow any understanding to be established. Repeat visits may be more positive in this context. Visitors, especially those on day visits, have temporal constraints and become intolerant of 'wasting time', for example in finding somewhere to park. Spontaneity may break down as 'hospitality' becomes a repetitive transaction for the host. For example, the regular, say half hour, repeat of the same commentary from the open topped buses which are now common in UK historic centres, can become a source of irritation to the local residents. Socio-cultural impacts may also vary according to the nature of the tourist, the extent of participation of local residents in the benefits of tourism, the rate of growth of tourism, the absolute numbers of tourists in relation to the host population, and the extent of differences (in, for example, wealth and behaviour) between visitors and hosts (Haukeland, 1984; Smith, 1977). Lundgren (1982, in Pearce 1992) observes: 'the force of tourist generated local impact seems to increase with the distance from the generating country'; this is a very debatable assertion but in some cases may be true.

Social costs, of relevance to historic centres in Europe, may include: a shift in local population and employment structures, with more young people, more females and more part-time employment; pressure on local services, such as public transport; an increase in crime; and antagonism between local people and visitors (Ryan, 1993; Brayley, 1990). Another very important social dimension is the extent to which non local investment can reduce control over local resources, as Krippendorf (1987) notes: 'Why has the loss of local autonomy - certainly the most negative long term effect of tourism - been practically ignored? Why does the local population tolerate it?' A local resident may also suffer a loss of sense of place, as his/her surroundings are transformed to accommodate the requirements of tourism. However, there may also be considerable social benefits, including a heightened sense of pride in one's own city, a broadening of understanding between hosts and visitors - with a softening of language, social, religious and nationality barriers. Local people may also gain considerably from the maintenance, or improvement, of various local services, for example for entertainment and health, than would have been possible without the tourist market.

Cultural problems may include the commercialisation of culture, religion and the arts, with the misuse of indigenous culture as tourist attractions, folkloreism, staged 'authenticity' (Cohen, 1979) and the undermining of traditional craft industries with cheaper, artificial imports. A process of acculturation may affect the host location, with the breaking down of local values, norms and traditions, in the face of a dominant and often richer flow of visitors. Language presents a particular sensitive issue (Prentice, 1993; ECTRC, 1988). But again it is easy to accentuate the negative, and eliminate the positive. There are cultural benefits and intercultural communication between hosts and visitors can improve understanding. Without visitors, local culture and traditions may have been lost completely, as might the market for traditional products.

Some 'models' of socio-cultural impacts suggest a one way ticket for the host area. Doxey's (1975) model, from his Niagara-on-the-Lake (Ontario, Canada) studies, partly falls into this category. The resident response shifts from euphoria to apathy to irritation to antagonism and finally to xenophobia. Yet it needn't be one way, such responses can and do happen, as illustrated by Bjorkland and Philbrick (1972), who argue that resident responses can vary considerably according to who gains and who loses (see Figure 3.3). This model is as applicable to groups within historic centres, as it is to groups of nations.

Physical impacts

Much of the discussion of the impacts of tourism on the physical environment traditionally focuses on the natural environment (Cohen, 1978; Romeril, 1989; Farrell and Runyan, 1991). Whilst this is significant for historic towns and cities, the impacts on the built environment can be equally important (Briassoulis and van der Straaten, 1992). Key dimensions of the natural environment include air and water quality, flora and fauna, and landscape; the built environment includes individual buildings, 'quarters' and the broader urban morphology of a location.

Large numbers of visitors may bring many problems for the environment. These can include pedestrian and vehicle congestion, with noise, air and water pollution, litter, trampling of vegetation, erosion of the physical fabric of buildings, inappropriate new buildings and land uses, insensitive rehabilitation of heritage sites and, at its extreme, the overwhelming of the morphology of a town. OECD studies (1981; and in Pearce, 1989) identify a range of 'stressor activities' and the 'environmental stress' which can result. Key stressor activities include major construction activities, generation of waste residuals, tourist activities and the effects on population dynamics. The ETB 'Tourism and the Environment' Working Group on Heritage Sites (ETB, 1991) highlights the problems which come from overcrowding, wear and tear, traffic congestion and parking, the provision of visitor facilities and changes in the character of localities. These can include a range of impacts: for example an increased risk of fire, pilferage, graffiti, accident risks from cars, atmospheric pollution, impaired ambience, destruction of architectural and archaeological integrity - and a tendency to 'trinketisation' or 'tweeness'. The ETB 'Tourism and Environment' Working Group on Historic Towns (ETB, 1991) highlights traffic congestion and parking; the congestion, noise, pollution and resident hostility created by coach tours; crowds and queues of pedestrians; and the provision of maintenance and infrastructure to meet the needs of visitors, viz:

Figure 3.3   Bjorklund and Philbrick model of social impacts

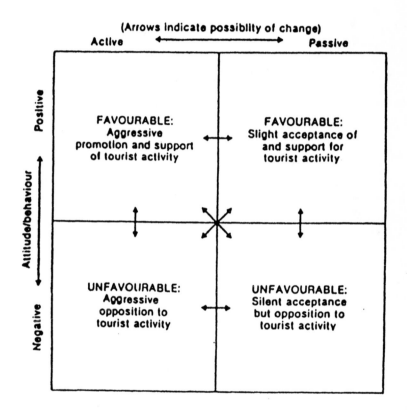

Source: Bjorklund and Philbrick, 1972

In Canterbury, the pressure of visitors involves the city council sweeping the city twice as many times as would be expected in a similar sized town without tourists. There are twice as many litter bins provided and public toilets require cleaning more frequently. (ETB, 1991)

There may, however, be many counterbalancing attributes. Tourism demand may bring the renewal of formerly derelict sites, and the resources to maintain historic buildings for the benefit of both local residents and tourists. It may create a heightened awareness of valued environments - highlighted for example with specialist architectural and ecology trails through the historic centres, festivals and other events. Visitor interest, concern and money can help the preservation of individual buildings for future generations. Visitor demand for heritage experiences, noted in the previous chapter, can stimulate the renovation of derelict historic buildings for use as attractions, restaurants and shops, as for example with the Albert Dock in Liverpool. The provision of additional services for visitors, such as better signing, street lighting, the provision and emptying of litter bins, street benches and facilities for the disabled, can also benefit the host community.

Budowski (1976) suggests that the relationship between tourism and the physical environment may be of three types: conflict, coexistence and symbiosis. Conflict is self explanatory; coexistence is where tourism and environmental conservation can exist side-by-side and with little interaction; symbiosis is where tourism and environmental conservation can be mutually supportive and beneficial. Under symbiosis, tourists benefit from the visitor experience and the environment enjoys improvements in management practices.

3.4 Tourism impacts: other dimensions

The impacts of an action are those resultant changes in environmental parameters, in space and time, compared with what would have happened without the action. The traditional approach is to analyse tourism impacts by economic, social and physical types - using parameters such as jobs, crime, air quality and litter. There are, however, other dimensions to impacts and these are briefly noted here (see Glasson *et al*, 1994).

Tourism may have immediate and direct impacts that give rise to secondary and indirect impacts over time. For example, if the immediate impact is traffic congestion, an indirect impact may be a decline in the attraction of the historic centre as a location for non-tourism related commercial activities. Impacts also have a spatial dimensions. One distinction is between local and strategic, with the latter covering impacts affecting areas beyond the immediate locality. This can be significant with regard to capacity issues, for whilst several small towns in an area may operate within their individual road network capacities, a key strategic link road serving them all may be over capacity at peak times.

Heritage resources cannot always be replaced; once destroyed, some may be lost forever. The distinction between reversible and irreversible impacts is a very important one. It may be possible to substitute, compensate for, or reconstruct a lost resource in some cases, but substitutions are rarely ideal. Some impacts (especially economic) can be quantified, others (especially social) are less tangible; the latter should not be ignored. Nor should the distributional impacts of tourism, and tourism developments, be ignored. Impacts do not fall evenly on affected parties and areas; there may be a net benefit to a location, but some groups and/or geographical areas may be receiving the bulk of the costs, with the main benefits going to others elsewhere. There is also the distinction between actual and perceived impacts. In some cases, tourists may be the easy scapegoat targets for the problems of an area which are only partly, or not, associated with tourism. Yet individual 'subjective' perceptions of impacts may be significant in influencing the responses and decisions of individuals towards tourism actions. They constitute an important source of information to be considered alongside more 'objective' predictions of impacts.

3.5 Environmental impact assessment

Increasing concern over the impacts of tourism, and of other development actions, has been paralleled by a growth in relevant planning and management tools. Environmental impact assessment (EIA) constitutes one such tool in good currency. It does have considerable relevance for tourism developments, and indeed for tourism as a policy direction for historic centres, although its application to date in such contexts has been limited.

EIA is a systematic process, that examines the environmental consequences of development actions in advance; it is a good example of the precautionary principle. EIA can be an important instrument for sustainable development; it can also help to improve decision making on a project, and can improve the design of new developments, indicating areas where the project can be modified to minimise or eliminate adverse impacts on the environment.

EIA was first formally established in the USA in 1969, with the National Environmental Policy Act (NEPA). In Europe, a 1985 European Community Directive on EIA 85/337 (CEC, 1985), provided the impetus, and introduced broadly uniform requirements for the countries of the Economic Union. The EU Directive indicates the broad steps involved in the EIA process, with a focus on development projects. The Directive also clarifies for which projects

EIA is mandatory (Annex 1) and for which it is discretionary (Annex 2). The detailed implementation of this framework Directive was left to individual Member States. In the UK, the Directive is implemented through 20 different sets of regulations. Most of the developments listed in the EU Directive Annexes 1 and 2 fall under the remit of the planning system, and are covered by the Town and Country Planning (Assessment of Environmental Effects) Regulations 1988. Under these regulations, tourism projects come under Schedule 2 - 'types of development which require environmental assessment if they are likely to have significant effects on the environment by virtue of factors such as their nature, size or location'. Tourism projects are normally covered under Schedule 2.10(b) 'an urban development project', and/or Schedule 2.11(a) 'a holiday village or hotel complex'.

The EIA process involves a number of steps as outlined in Figure 3.4. These are not detailed here and the reader should refer to relevant texts (Glasson et al, 1994; Wathern, 1988; DoE, 1989). Although the steps are outlined in linear fashion in the figure, EIA is best registered as a cyclical activity, with feedback and interaction between the steps in the process. Approximately 300 EISs have been produced annually in the UK since 1988; the bulk have been for Schedule 2 projects, and include several for leisure and tourism projects.

However, the EIA process is not without its problems. These relate to the limited coverage of socio-economic impacts in many assessments, weak impact prediction methods, limited or no public participation, and the absence, or limited, monitoring of impacts after a development goes ahead. In addition, one of the most significant limitations, of particular relevance to tourism, is the limited focus on projects.

There is a need for strategic environmental assessment (SEA), expanding EIA from projects to programmes, plans and policies (PPPs), for example for a road programme for a region, a structure plan for an English county, or a tourism policy for a historic city. SEA represents a logical extension of project assessment. It can cope better with cumulative impacts, such as the accumulated traffic impacts of the development of several tourist attractions in a location, and can better address alternatives and mitigation measures than project assessment. SEA systems already exist in limited forms in California and the Netherlands, and to a lesser extent in Canada, Germany and New Zealand (Therivel et al, 1992). The EU Fifth Action Programme on the Environment states: 'Given the goal of achieving sustainable development, it seems only logical, if not essential, to apply an assessment of the environmental implications of all relevant policies, plans and programmes' CEC, 1992). But the implementation of SEA is fraught with both technical and procedural problems. On the technical side, alternatives can be diffuse, information limited, and there are few successful case studies. In the policy

Figure 3.4   Important steps in the EIA process

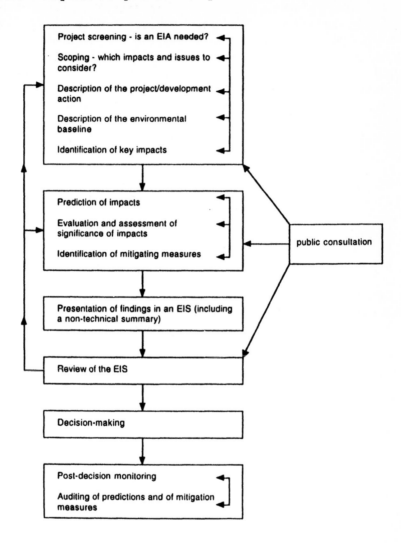

Source: Glasson et al, 1994

making process, many PPPs are nebulous and evolve in an incremental and unclear fashion, so there is no clear time when their environmental impacts can be assessed. PPPs do not have clear boundaries at which they stop and other policies begin. Nevertheless, under the UK Department of Environment Planning Policy Guidance note 12 (DoE, 1992), there are signs of progress in the development of SEA in the UK planning system. PPG12 requires the environmental appraisal of local and structure plans; such plans relate, *inter alia*, to historic towns and cities, and may include tourism policies.

3.6 Conclusions

The growing awareness of the significance of tourism impacts and the development of assessment methods is encouraging. However, isolating the impacts does raise conceptual and technical problems: what would have happened to the historic centre without tourism; how do we trade off the economic impact apples, social impact oranges and physical impact bananas! Do we have adequate baseline data on the various dimensions of the environment in our historic centres? The methods and approaches of EIA are valuable for new projects, but by definition much of the tourism infrastructure of historic centres, including of course the key heritage components, is already in place. In such situations visitor impact management measures become more appropriate. SEA relating to the overall tourism policy/strategy may be more relevant for many centres. However policies need to be assessed against objectives, and against indicators. It is in this context that the issue of carrying capacity, in relation to factors such as air quality, noise, traffic congestion and resident acceptability, comes into play. The identification of capacities is not easy and is controversial; the following chapter provides a pathway through the carrying capacity field.

4 Tourism carrying capacity

4.1 Introduction

Recently, in response to the negative effects of tourism, real or otherwise, business leaders, politicians and academics alike have argued that without a more 'sustainable' approach to tourism development it is probable that the 'environment', in all its forms, will be despoiled at an ever increasing rate (Globe, 1990). Central to many arguments in support of sustainability is a reference to 'capacity'. As an element of sustainability, carrying capacity is said to represent an approach to tourism management where levels of visitor activity or development in a destination are maintained within acceptable limits. This reference to 'acceptable limits', however, represents the key difficulty with operationalising 'capacity' in a practical management setting. While many in government and industry espouse the virtues of capacity in limiting negative impacts, they do so with little understanding of what this means in terms of policy and action.

Tourism is, by its very nature, an agent of change. Some impacts of change may be controlled, regulated or directed. If properly managed, tourism has the potential of being a renewable industry, where resource integrity is maintained or even enhanced. If mis-managed, or allowed to expand within short-term goals and objectives, it has the capability of destroying the very resources upon which it is built. In its most basic form, carrying capacity represents a 'maximum sustainable yield,' inferring awareness of both the costs and benefits of tourism. Like sustainable tourism development, it is difficult to disagree with, but questions such as 'what is acceptable?', 'who says so?' and 'on what authority do they make these judgements?', often go unanswered.

Despite these issues, carrying capacity has received renewed endorsement as a guiding principle in tourism management. However, not all who support it understand or appreciate the complexity or comprehensive analysis required to translate the concept into practical management. Thus, despite its inherent appeal, as witnessed in the accumulation of literature on the subject (Williams and Gill, 1991), carrying capacity tends to remain ill-defined, mishandled and in some cases, stimulates a mixed debate as to its usefulness as a management tool. Instead of carrying capacity *per se*, many now choose to utilize concepts such as the 'limits of acceptable change' (LAC) and 'visitor impact management' (VIM) as means of addressing ever-increasing visitor numbers and their concomitant impact on destinations. As will be discussed later, the LAC and VIM concepts tend to build on the notion of a carrying capacity, but use it more as an underlying philosophy, rather than the source of some mythical value.

4.2 The origins of carrying capacity

The notion of carrying capacity has its origins in the field of wildlife management. Here capacity was discussed in terms of the maximum number of grazing animals which could be maintained on a site in 'good flesh', without causing damage to their food supply, or the soil (Wall, 1982). Adapted by outdoor recreation managers in the early 1960s, 'capacity' was used to determine the maximum number of people who could use a recreation area without destroying its essential qualities (Wager, 1964). Carrying capacities were developed and set in management strategies to try and influence social and environmental impacts of recreation activity in various outdoor settings.

Most early definitions suggested that carrying capacity was the "level of recreational use an area (could) withstand while providing a sustained quality of recreation, a quality environment and a quality recreational experience" (Wager, 1964). Similarly, it was considered to be "that character of use that could be specified over time, by an area's development at a certain level, without causing excessive damage to either the environment or the experience of the visitor" (Lime and Stankey, 1971). A decade later, Mathieson and Wall (1982) similarly re-defined capacity as "the maximum number of people who could use a site without unacceptable alteration in the physical environment and without an unacceptable decline in the quality of the experience gained by visitors".

Implicit in these, and other early, definitions was the recognition of two fundamental components of carrying capacity: a quality environment, and a quality visitor experience (Graefe, 1989; Kuss *et al*, 1990). Discussions in the literature examined: 'ecological capacity', primarily concerned with the impact of recreational use on flora and fauna; 'physical capacity' which examined space requirements for different kinds and levels of outdoor recreational activities; 'social capacity' which considered the relationship between the visitor experience and the quality and quantity of their interaction with other visitors to the same recreation site; and 'facility capacity' which was primarily concerned with construction and development guidelines for visitor facilities in the recreational setting (see Williams and Gill, 1991). All of these, however, tended to look at one aspect of capacity in relative isolation. Thus, while the ability of one sector, or setting, to absorb visitor activity may have been determined, others received only cursory acknowledgment, or were ignored altogether.

In an attempt to overcome many of these difficulties of single sector analysis, Lindsay (1986:17) combined these elements to re-define carrying capacity as the "physical, biological, social and psychological capacity of the ... environment to support tourist activity without diminishing environmental quality or visitor satisfaction". By taking account of these various dimensions, he suggested the concept of capacity was best explained by the formula:

$$CC = f \ (Q, \ T, \ N, \ U, \ DM, \ AB)$$

with the *carrying capacity* (CC) of a setting represented as a function of:

- the **Quantity** of resources available;
- the **Tolerance** of those resources to visitor use;
- the actual **Number** of visitors at the site or setting;
- the type of **Use** or visitor activity undertaken;
- the **Design** and **Management** of visitor facilities in the setting;
- and the **Attitude** and **Behaviour** of visitors on the site, and similarly of the 'site' managers.

In the recreation and wildlife management fields, an extensive literature on carrying capacity has developed, and it is from these natural resource management discussions that the concept has spread to an idea of a 'tourism carrying capacity'. However, key problems remain with many early definitions and their subsequent tourism translations. Although capacity was seen in terms of several factors (i.e. ecological, physical, social and facilities), research and debate on these topics have been limited to variations on the theme of visitor impacts on the physical environment (Mathieson and Wall, 1982), or social interaction (Kuss *et al*, 1990). They have tended to focus on the relationship between physical amenity and user satisfaction, to the virtual exclusion of other factors, including the economic, cultural and political dimensions of tourism and of its impacts.

4.3 Tourism carrying capacity: problems and prospects

From its inception as a site management tool, carrying capacity has evoked mixed feelings and continues to frustrate precise definition. Although not claiming to be exhaustive, Getz (1982, 1983) identified as many as six different overall approaches which have been used to define or delimit the tourism carrying capacity of a destination. Indeed, it has been suggested that there are almost as many definitions of capacity as there are people who have written on the subject (Wall, 1982). To some it has come to represent a method of analysis, supporting management actions which limit undesirable impacts; for others it may be the threshold level beyond which negative factors start to operate (WTO, 1985). Others consider it to be neither absolute nor readily measurable, and believe the pursuit of some 'numeric' value of little use, particularly when no further action is taken once the 'capacity' has been determined (Washburne, 1982; Bury, 1976; Shelby and Heberlein, 1986).

In its most simplified form O'Reilly (1986) states that capacity has been defined as the "maximum number of tourists who can be contained in a certain destination area". Similarly, Costa (1991) suggests that carrying capacity is the "maximum number of visitors beyond which the costs of tourism growth more than offset its benefits". These definitions imply some sort of 'physical limit', or absolute value, to which tourism activity and associated development approach with impunity, but exceed at peril. Essentially this approach looks for a 'numeric' indicator which will describe the time when a destination area has reached its capacity 'ceiling'. The literature abounds with similar discussions on 'tourism carrying capacity', describing various threshold indicators in terms of volume, density or market-mix (Figure 4.1).

Although it is this 'numeric' approach which has received the most attention by some researchers, it is also one which is repudiated by others in the tourism field who see it simply as 're-inventing the wheel', already rejected by our colleagues in recreation and wildlife management as unworkable (Bury, 1976; Washburne, 1982; Williams and Gill, 1991).

A key failing with many past (and particularly 'numeric' based) definitions of capacity has been in their search and application of supposed 'ceiling' values to pragmatic management strategies and action. In many cases, the development of some 'absolute' value has represented the end process of capacity analysis, with little, if any, further practical application to affect visitor impacts. Upon defining the capacity of the setting, further action has not been forthcoming because the 'capacity gurus' failed to see the wider context of the tourism system, and the problems of implementation. As Schneider *et al* (1978:180) state, "a major shortcoming in most ... management plans is the lack of objectives that allow managers to explicitly state the conditions they seek and to measure performance with regard to achieving these objectives". Now, many are beginning to recognise that carrying capacity is meaningless without the prior specification of goals and objectives to guide management activity. Thus it is argued that once the 'capacity' has been determined, it must be followed by pre-determined actions to mitigate or ameliorate the situation. Virtually all relevant articles on the subject suggest that carrying capacity is not some absolute value just waiting to be discovered, but a range of values which must be related to specific management objectives in any given area (Kuss et al, 1990).

Figure 4.1   Indicators of carrying capacity

Threshold Identification	Threshold Examples
VOLUME	peak, hourly, daily, weekly, yearly volumes of various types of visitors (eg. bed-nights, visits, visitor days, etc.)
DENSITY	number of persons/hectare for different activities at different locations (eg. visitors /hectare of beach, tourists/sq.m of restaurant, shop space, etc.)
MARKET MIX	number of visitor units relative to resident units (eg visitor/resident population; visitor beds/resident beds; visitor use of public facilities/resident use of public facilities.

Source: Williams and Gill, 1991

A second problem identified by Williams and Gill (1991) concerns the lack of evidence in the literature which supports the argument that by simply lowering, or indeed raising, any one of the 'capacity thresholds' listed in Figure 4.1, there will necessarily be a predictable change in a destination's ability to absorb tourism. The pursuit of a tourism carrying capacity by some has been with little, if any, empirical evidence that by simply identifying a threshold level, current and future impacts can be controlled. Shelby and Heberlein (1986) suggest that in determining the carrying capacity of a setting there are two further issues which need to be considered: management parameters and impact parameters. The former concerns those elements of tourism which an agency can directly manipulate in management activity; the

47

latter concerns the outcome or effect of visitor-use on either the environment or the visitors themselves. Although there is a certain amount of literature available which describes the impacts of tourism in various settings, the manipulation of tourist flows, lengths of stay, or the type of tourist is often beyond the control (or even understanding) of destination tourism agencies. Although this does not refute the value of the carrying capacity concept for management activity, the claims that it will solve all the industry's problems has primarily evolved from a misunderstanding of the nature of tourism, of tourist destinations, and of use-impact relationships.

A third fundamental problem with the use of carrying capacity in tourism planning and management is that any one site, or destination, has one inherent use level or maximum absolute capacity (Wall, 1982; Bury, 1976; O'Reilly, 1986). This is simply not the case. As Wall (1982) suggests, a site designated for some special scientific interest may only be able to maintain a low user threshold before degradation of the original qualities begins to appear. That same site if designated for concentrated development may accommodate a significantly higher user-density before negative effects begin to emerge. Notwithstanding the other issues and arguments involved, this point is evidenced in the development of Disney World in Florida. The original site where this facility is located could not withstand the levels of visitation it currently receives without severe environmental consequences and hence would have a very low visitor threshold. The same site managed as it is and including its structural modifications, has a very high user-threshold and high visitor throughput with little effect on the immediate setting. This suggests that pre-determined objectives and site modification can alter the carrying capacity of any given setting.

A fourth major problem with capacity has been in the use of visitor numbers as the critical factor. This suggests that as numbers increase, crowding, congestion and other related impacts automatically develop until the capacity is reached and perhaps exceeded. To many, this represents an over-simplified view of the effects of growing visitor numbers. While impacts do develop with the presence of tourists, the volume of visitors is but one factor. As the graphs in Figure 4.2 suggest, increasing visitor numbers have a variable effect on visitor satisfaction, which depends on the site in question and the situation under analysis. In fact, studies have shown that there is only a tenuous relationship between actual visitor numbers, and the quality of the visitor experience (Veal, 1973; Hall, 1974; Wager, 1964). Visitor densities are relatively unimportant, or are meaningful only when analyzed in concert with other variables (Kuss et al, 1990). Each destination is unique, and it is the type of activity, the timing of such activity, group size and composition, visitor expectations and the site's own characteristics, which influence perceptions of crowding, satisfaction, or other negative impacts, as much as actual numbers.

It is a combination of these factors which create site-specific responses, which in turn are not readily generalized to other visitor settings. In broad terms, the carrying capacity of a setting or destination will be influenced by two key elements (Mathieson and Wall, 1982):

- the tourist's characteristics; and

- the destination area's and local population's characteristics.

Although much previous analysis of capacity has considered these elements, it has done so from a limited perspective whilst drawing very broad generalisations and assumptions. Tourists, and the multitude of current destinations, are not uniform and the application of carrying capacity in tourism management and planning will need to take account of these differences. As noted in Chapter 3, whether as individuals or in groups, tourists vary in terms of personal socio-economic attributes (age, sex, disposable income, etc); have differing travel motivations, expectations and time available; and varying ethnic, religious and behavioral patterns. Equally significant is the recognition that individuals and groups of tourists react differently to visitor density, type of activity, and length of stay. All of these elements have a role to play in determining the impact of tourism on any destination. Their inclusion in capacity analysis, however, has proven difficult because of this diversity, and for the most part has received very little in-depth analysis.

Tourist destinations and their population characteristics are equally complex. Relevant variables include: the natural environment (bio-physical processes and local geography); the economic structure (investment, location and diversity); social structures (demographics, culture and quality of life); political organisations (structure, regulations and principles); and the level of tourist development in the destination (ownership, quality, and rate of development) (e.g. Mathieson and Wall, 1982). Each of these variables also has some part to play in determining the tourism carrying capacity of a destination. Research has considered some aspects of these variables, but rarely have they been examined in a collective fashion. It is the interrelationship between them which is perhaps most important in helping us to better understand carrying capacity, particularly if it is to be meaningful and applied effectively to planning and management activity.

4.4 Tourism carrying capacity: towards a better understanding

Williams and Gill (1994) suggest that although most previous discussions of carrying capacity have all had their own particular bias, they have also based their rationale on four key elements:

Figure 4.2 User satisfaction and level of use

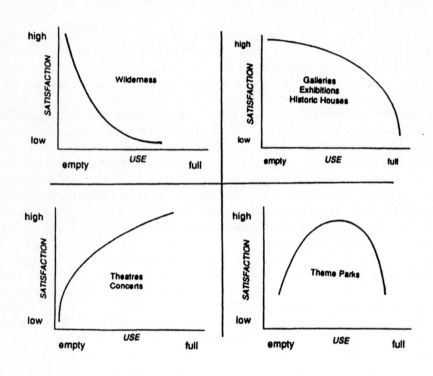

(after Veal, 1973; Hall, 1974; Wager, 1964)

- tourism in its various forms is a catalyst for change, and brings with it the potential for economic, social and environmental benefits and costs;

- desired conditions can be identified for tourism, beyond which tourism is not sustainable for local populations, visitors, or both;

• these desired conditions are not fixed, but vary geographically and temporally depending upon local economic, social, political and environmental circumstances, as well as the understanding of tourism's influence upon local conditions; and

• management strategies can be established and implemented that are capable of controlling the rate and direction of change/impact introduced by tourism, in keeping with desired conditions.

Thus the concept of a tourism carrying capacity does have its merits, but it is the traditional focus of trying to determine some absolute or limiting value from one point of view which has done little to progress its application in terms of impact resolution (Williams and Gill, 1991 and 1994). As Figure 4.3 suggests, tourism carrying capacity is really a network, or web, of all these tourism elements, split between 'hard', objective, or quantifiable dimensions and 'soft' or more subjective, qualitative perspectives. The more quantifiable aspects concern ecology, economics and physical space and infrastructure; the more qualitative elements concern the real and perceived influence of tourism activity on the interrelationship between 'hosts and guests', and the 'managers' willingness or ability to actually control the other five elements. In addition, each of these may vary over space and time, while affecting the significance of any one, or all capacity attributes. In turn, each segment or subsystem of this 'capacity web' can be described in terms of its own capacity attributes.

Dimensions of tourism carrying capacity

(i)   the *ecological* dimension of tourism carrying capacity relates the ability of the natural environment to respond to tourist use. It describes the effects of visitor activity on flora, fauna, soils, air and water quality in a destination. This ecological element is best reflected in the work of the recreation managers concerning tolerance levels of natural environments to sustained visitor use. Examples of breaches of the ecological capacity include: the disappearance of wildlife due to visitor presence, the trampling of plant species, and the visual erosion of landscapes due to excessive human use;

(ii)   the *physical* dimension of tourism carrying capacity is primarily concerned with the basic infrastructure and facilities available in a destination. It describes such aspects as the quality and quantity of water supplies, sewerage capacity, energy supplies, parking availability,

Figure 4.3 The capacity network or capacity web

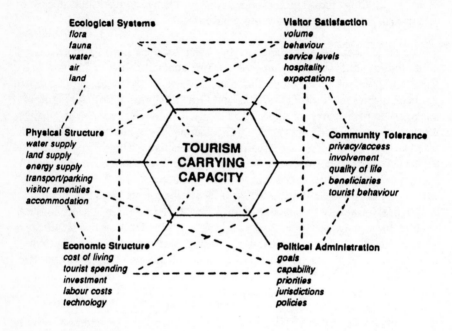

DIMENSIONS   PERSPECTIVES

Ecological Systems
flora
fauna
water
air
land

Visitor Satisfaction
volume
behaviour
service levels
hospitality
expectations

Physical Structure
water supply
land supply
energy supply
transport/parking
visitor amenities
accommodation

TOURISM CARRYING CAPACITY

Community Tolerance
privacy/access
involvement
quality of life
beneficiaries
tourist behaviour

Economic Structure
cost of living
tourist spending
investment
labour costs
technology

Political Administration
goals
capability
priorities
jurisdictions
policies

(after Williams and Gill, 1991)

local transportation issues, accommodation provision and other visitor services and attractions. Physical capacity relates the impact of increased demand and greater visitor numbers to the ability of these services to operate efficiently. Examples where visitor numbers have produced a service overload include periodic water shortages, sewerage failures, excess traffic congestion and local energy shortages;

(iii)   the *economic* dimension of tourism carrying capacity concerns the destination's ability to absorb tourist functions without squeezing out other desirable local activities. This is often referred to as 'crowding out' where the profitability of tourism firms becomes much higher than other normal urban functions, with the latter being shifted to more peripheral, or less expensive, locations. In addition, economic capacity also concerns the seasonality of tourism and the effect this has on the labour force and general economy of the destination. Examples of when the economic capacity of a destination has been exceeded include the replacement of local service shops (e.g. grocers, butchers) by souvenir shops and cafes, significant changes in local employment levels corresponding to the tourist season, the importation of 'foreign' labour to meet tourist demand, and swings in local economic prosperity corresponding to trends in tourist demand.

Perspectives of tourism carrying capacity

(iv)   the *community* or *social* aspect of tourism carrying capacity concerns a destination's ability to absorb tourism without negative effects being perceived by *local residents*. Destinations vary in their collective tolerance of visitors which, like 'visitor' capacity, can change both seasonally and spatially. Community capacity describes the degree of tolerance or acceptance, of tourism by local residents, in relation to the effects tourism has on their quality of life. Key issues concern levels of privacy, aspects of visitor behaviour, the level of contact between residents and tourists, and the distribution of benefits. Situations when a community's tolerance of tourism has been overstepped include a general annoyance and dislike of tourists because of congestion, noise, crowding in the community and culturally unacceptable behaviour, exploitation of tourists through excessively inflated prices, and in the extreme, an outright aggression and physical abuse of tourists;

(v)   the *visitor* or *tourist* aspect of tourism carrying capacity considers those factors which influence visitor satisfaction in a destination. It describes the ability of a destination to provide a quality visitor experience in relation to increasing visitor numbers. Each individual varies in his/her preference for density of use, which is primarily dependent on the type of interaction desired for different activities at different times (Wager, 1964; Bury, 1976). Visitor capacity is the point where, for any number of reasons, there is an identifiable decrease in market demand. A few examples of when the visitor's capacity has been exceeded include a general shift towards a more gregarious tourist market, declining standards of service and amenity, and a shrinking tourist season;

(vi)   finally, the *political capacity* or *management capability* of a destination focuses on the organisational ability of a destination to co-ordinate and direct local tourism management. Tourism is a highly fragmented industry, speaking with no single authority. The political capacity of a destination is thus represented in the level of co-operation evident between the public and private sectors, the level of local resident involvement in the decision process, as well as the level of understanding of current market composition, market trends, and market satisfaction. This is reflected in the presence, or absence, of adequate policies to effectively manage the local tourism industry. It also concerns the industry's willingness, or competence, to look beyond short-term goals, and establish long-term objectives to regulate and control the five other capacity elements. Examples of a political *in*ability include destinations with market-led local tourism industries, with products developed solely to meet a real or potential tourist demand, local policies and tourism strategies dominated by promotional and marketing issues, and a dis-jointed supply of tourist services and facilities.

Each element of the capacity network may not have the same magnitude in every destination. In some locations the economic aspect may be the limiting factor where the development of tourism may require such high levels of imports that there would be no financial benefit to the destination, elsewhere the host acceptance of tourists and their reaction to visitors may determine whether or not that destination will part of a tourist product. While any one of these aspects of the 'capacity web' may play a more prominent role than the others, each must be considered in the overall tourism carrying capacity of a destination. In terms of a general formula, tourism carrying capacity is perhaps better defined as a function of these various dimensions and perspectives of the capacity web, with:

$$TCC = f \text{ (Ecol, Phys, Econ) (TC, RA, Pol)}$$

where *tourism carrying capacity (TCC)* becomes a function of the:

ecological systems in a destination;
physical infrastructure and tourist facility development;
economic characteristics of tourist investment and expenditure;
tourists' characteristics in social-cultural and behavioural terms;
residents' acceptance or tolerance of tourism activity; and
political capability and authority to take effective management decisions.

It is the magnitude and direction of impacts on each of these subsystems which defines the ability of a destination to absorb tourism activity, where the marginal benefits of providing for the tourist continues to exceed, or a least equal, the marginal costs.

4.5 Towards better management

A number of authors suggest that the determination of capacity requires two separate elements, a *descriptive component* which examines the relationship between specific conditions of use and the impacts associated with these conditions; and an *evaluative component* which incorporates value judgements on the acceptability of these various impacts (Shelby and Heberlein, 1984, 1986; Williams and Gill, 1991). In some cases the evaluation of impacts is relatively simple, based on expert judgement or regulations. As is often the case in tourism settings, the social/community and visitor elements are more difficult to define. Unfortunately the contrast between impact and evaluation are often confused in the literature (Wight, 1994). It must be recognised that the introduction of tourism in any a setting will bring about change.

A problem with many previous attempts to examine and define carrying capacity in terms of tourism has been that this effort has often represented an end in itself. A number of examples in the literature define 'carrying capacities' in specific settings, but they do not then describe what, if anything, has been the result of their 'discovery'. In addition, these studies have also represented a 'snapshot' of issues at one point in time which may not reflect the dynamic nature of the tourism system. These difficulties with the application of capacity are not surprising, given that the original concept was designed to examine wildlife management issues which have a more precise and often measurable application (Wight, 1994). Subsequent translation for tourism development has added numerous variables, inherent to man-made systems, which "suggest an objectivity and precision that is not warranted by its use in the planning community" (Wight, 1994:3). As McCool (1991) suggests, the concept of carrying capacity in guiding tourism development has met with limited success because it cannot deal with the complexity and diversity of the industry. If we are to manage this change brought about by tourism, then many now argue that the use of carrying capacity in attempt to manipulate use levels is in error. Instead it is suggested that we should use the concept to underpin tourism development and management, but based on detailed objectives and evaluation of tourism impacts engendered through the adaptation of such frameworks as the *Limits of Acceptable Change* (LAC) and *Visitor Impact Management* (VIM).

Instead of trying to establish a finite and predictable link between use level and impact (which is the basis of carrying capacity), a more useful approach may be to assess the likely impact of an activity on the destination; agree in advance what degree of change will be tolerated; monitor the industry on a regular and systematic basis; and decide what actions will be taken if these 'quality standards' are exceeded. This is the basis of the Limits of Acceptable Change (LAC) approach which identifies resource and social conditions in a given setting and defines management techniques which will maintain these conditions over time. It avoids the outright establishment of use-limits, or the type and scale of development which can take place, but rather seeks to understand the change we are willing to accept as stewards of the environment. Originally developed by the US Forest Service (see Stankey *et al*, 1985) this approach recognises that the evaluation of impacts is a matter for managerial judgement, and that such judgements should be based on an informed assessment of social, economic and environmental values, as well as resource sustainability, and user reaction (Sidaway, 1991).

In the recreation setting, the LAC management process sets out a series of nine sequential steps (see Figure 4.4) which broadly help to identify acceptable social and resource characteristics of the setting, compare existing conditions with those desired, identify a series of possible actions which will help achieve these desired conditions; and establish systematic and regular measurement techniques to monitor change and effectiveness of management actions undertaken (Sidaway, 1991; Wight, 1994). Williams and Gill (1991) suggest the LAC approach is of particular value for tourism development and management. It helps to identify a logical sequence of steps that leads to the development of management standards for tourism settings in social and environmental terms. It recognises that some impacts created by tourism are inevitable, and that there may be several standards and indicators needed to handle these different impacts. It requires the setting of objectives, indicators and quality standards prior to development, with specific desirable management objectives used as the means to define unacceptable impacts.

However, the LAC approach is not without its difficulties (Wight, 1994) and unless detailed information can be collected on all the aspects of the 'capacity web' to fit into the LAC process for each destination, there is the very real threat of 'quality standards' being adopted arbitrarily, or at such a low level, that they may not be able to identify long-term and cumulative impacts. In addition, it is argued that the basis of the LAC approach (as distinct from capacity analysis) is that it is part of an ongoing process of planning, managing and monitoring. If it is only used as a 'one-off' tool in terms of appeasement, or meeting environmental regulations at one point in time, then it will have little use in managing visitor impacts. As a result, McCool (1991) and Wight (1994) suggest that when this approach is applied to tourism it is more important to focus on the overall process of management and the desired end product, rather than adhering to these nine steps in strict fashion (see Figure 4.5).

Visitor Impact Management

Carrying capacity has, in most cases, taken a single sector approach to examining use-impact relationships. Biologists, ecologists and environmentalists have examined how levels of use may influence flora, fauna, and soil properties in different settings. Similarly sociologists, psychologists, and anthropologists have examined how visitor densities may affect the quality of the visitor experience, and the socio-cultural effects of foreign influence on local populations. Each of these disciplines has developed its own body of literature on these relationships, rarely, however, has any attention been placed on the integration of these findings across the various realms of research (Kuss *et al*, 1990).

Another perspective which builds on the general concept of capacity, but one that tries to integrate various disciplines, is the Visitor Impact Management approach (VIM). VIM is an approach which moves beyond the limits identified in ecological and social studies of carrying capacity and tries to apply to human impacts and interactions. VIM recognises that simply establishing limits may do little to reduce the impacts they were intended to resolve (Graefe *et al*, 1990). It is argued that, first, we need to better understand the nature of impacts and the factors related to their occurrence, and only then can we apply this to management strategies in attempt to reduce tourism impacts. As a sequential process similar to the LAC approach, VIM is a set of procedures which first reviews management objectives for tourism; then identifies indicators related to these management objectives (see Figure 4.6). Standards for these indicators are then selected which correspond to the management objectives. These standards are compared with existing conditions to look for specific problems, probable causes for the various impacts, and possible breaches of quality standards. Potential management strategies are devised which should lead to the mitigation of the impacts, and finally a continual monitoring process is devised which checks the effectiveness of management actions, so that the process becomes dynamic and able to respond to changing conditions of use and impact (Williams and Gill, 1991).

The relationship between use and impact is neither linear nor uniform, and five key principles have been identified in the literature which explain the

Figure 4.4 Limits of acceptable change planning process

1. Define Issues and Concerns
economic
social
environmental
political/institutional constraints

2. Define and Describe Opportunity Classes
resource
social
managerial

3. Select Indicators of Resource and Social Conditions
economic
social
environmental
political

4. Identify Existing Resource and Social Conditions
current status of indicators
standards data base

5. Specify Opportunity Class Standards
acceptable, observable, measurable limits

6. Identify Alternative Opportunity Class Allocations
type of use
location
timing

7. Identify Management Actions
direct
indirect

8. Evaluate and Select Alternative Management Actions
costs vs. benefits
consensus building
management capability

9. Implement and Monitor
compare against standards
adjust management strategies accordingly

(after Stankey *et al*, 1985)

Figure 4.5   The LAC process

The LAC Process

Issues
⇩
Goals   ↑
⇩   Continous
Standards   Public
⇩   Involvement
Inventory   in
⇩   Environmental
Actions   Analysis
⇩   ↓
Monitor

(after McCool, 1991; and Wight, 1994)

relationship between visitor use and impacts. It is the recognition and understanding of these interrelationships which, it is argued, need to figure prominently in the development of management strategies if the VIM process is to have any affect on impact mitigation (see Kuss *et al*, 1990). These are:

• there is no single predictable response between the use of a setting and the visitor/host experience. Tourists and hosts alike are affected by a series of interrelated impacts that result from visitor use of a setting. These lead to tangible social and environmental outcomes, which, in turn, lead to a variety of perceptual and behavioral responses by hosts and residents;

59

Figure 4.6 Examples of possible impact indicators

Physical Impacts	Biological Impacts	Social Impacts
number of social trails	soil fauna and microflora	number of visitors in area per day
visible erosion	ground cover density	by mode of transport
soil bulk density	percent loss of ground cover	number of groups in area per day
soil drainage	plant species composition	by mode of transport
soil compaction	plant species diversity	number of encounters
soil pH	proportion of exotic plant species	with other groups
soil productivity	plant height	by activity mode
amount of litter/ duff	selected plant species vigour	by mode of transport
depth of litter/duff	extent of diseased vegetation	by locations of encounter
area of barren core	extent of scarred or mutilated trees	by size of groups
area of bare ground	abundance of selected wildlife species	visitor perceptions of impact
area of complete campsite	presence/absence of selected wildlife species	on environment
number of fire rings	frequency of wildlife sightings	on crowding
size of fire rings	wildlife reproduction success	visitor satisfaction
		visitor reports of undesirable
		visitor behaviours
		amount of litter (trash) in area
		number of visitor complaints

(after Graefe *et al*, 1987, in Williams and Gill, 1991)

- most impacts do not exhibit a direct linear relationship with user density. User/impact relationships are affected by many factors and by the strength, frequency and nature of the interaction which varies widely for different situations;

- there is an inherent variation in the levels of tolerance between different groups in different settings. Individuals have differing desires; trying to place people into homogeneous groupings has proven difficult. Not everyone will respond in the same way to increasing visitor numbers, and while some may lose out, others may benefit from increased levels of visitation;

- some types of activity cause different impacts due to varying intensities of use, and visitor characteristics. Some types of activity generate impacts faster than others, and these can vary according to the type of tourist, modes of transport, visitor characteristics, numbers, and individual behaviour; and

- tourism impacts are also influenced by any number of site-specific and seasonal variables. Varying perceptions of both hosts and visitors may be affected by different types of settings in a destination, the time of interaction and seasonal variations.

Although not previously employed in a tourism context, Williams and Gill (1991:13) state that the process of Visitor Impact Management may be useful in helping planners and managers identify unacceptable tourism impacts, determine those factors most likely to be affecting the incidence and severity of those impacts and then select potential strategies to deal with them. However, like the LAC approach, the practical implementation of VIM in the tourism setting still has limitations.

In order to determine if 'quality standards' are not being met, it is necessary to have accurate information on the amount, type and distribution of visitors. Use measurements must go beyond simple area densities comparing number of hosts to number of visitors in any given area, and include visitor activities, length of stay, party size and spatial and temporal distribution (Kuss et al, 1990). Although this type of data may have little use outside the setting in which it is collected, it is argued this is precisely the type of data which is required to develop management strategies at the local level. It is evident from most previous studies that this level of analysis has rarely been undertaken. This limits the validity of findings for the better understanding of impacts in other settings. In addition, many of the impact relationships described above may change over time, or in response to other management actions (Greafe et al, 1990). Systematic monitoring and evaluation will be necessary to see what refinement of actions may be needed to maintain impacts at acceptable levels. Managing visitor impacts must begin with the setting of specific goals and objectives for the destination. Then appropriate indicators can be selected which will identify desired conditions of the social and environmental resource. In essence this is what Shelby and Heberlein (1986) termed their *evaluative component* of carrying capacity which, for the most part has been omitted from much tourism development and management activity.

4.6 Discussion and conclusions

A great deal of the research on carrying capacity suggests that, at the very least, this concept is difficult to define in any absolute sense, and as such has met with mixed results when expressed as a management tool. There are a number of reasons for this including unrealistic expectations of finding some absolute capacity value, untenable assumptions of use-impact relationships, skewed value judgements as to what is 'acceptable', and inadequate control mechanisms to ensure management objectives are achieved (Williams and Gill, 1991).

Carrying capacity is a relative management concept, or framework, it is not a scientific theory. The pre-occupation with finding some technique or method which would allow us to determine when a destination is full has been plagued with problems. Given the diversity and multiplicity of factors which affect the nature of capacity, this calculation would seem to be exceedingly difficult considering the many intangible qualities inherent in tourism carrying capacity (i.e. community perceptions, visitor satisfaction and political attitudes). There cannot be an unqualified, single, number which determines the optimal solution, as each situation would be unique in its response to visitor impacts in both space and time. There is no inherent carrying capacity of a destination, but rather a range of factors which depend on various management objectives. This is not to suggest that carrying capacity is meaningless, but rather that it needs to take account of many issues, as a means to an end and not, as it has been, as an end in itself.

One of the major building blocks in defining capacity has been the assumption of a direct relationship between levels of use and negative impact. Research has shown that the use-impact relationship is not as simple as the original carrying capacity concept implied or was assumed. It may be mediated by a variety of personal and situational factors. A common short-coming of capacity research is that it has typically considered only a subset of capacity attributes, which has then provided a false, or incomplete, picture of the full nature of tourism impacts. It is not possible to manage for a specified impact without a full (or better) understanding of how the parameters of that impact are affected by visitor use, or other capacity attributes. All elements of capacity are affected by a series of interrelated impacts which result from varying intensities of visitor use. In any one destination or situation, impacts may change through time and space. Where one impact may be accepted, another may break the tolerance barrier for any number of reasons. There cannot be a single predictable response to varying use levels.

Carrying capacity is not precise, as it requires both judgement and scientific theory. While many have tried to perfect the scientific side, the perceptions of 'hosts and guests' and the role of government in tourism capacity analysis has been rather neglected. This is partly because the scientific (or numeric) elements of capacity (i.e. economic, ecological and physical aspects) are more readily quantifiable, whereas socio-cultural perceptions and political agendas prove more difficult to add to the equation. Carrying capacity cannot be determined in the absence of value judgements which specify what levels of impact are acceptable, and under what conditions further tourism growth would become undesirable. The problem arises with the variety of opinions as to what is desirable, acceptable or appropriate in each situation. Differences occur both within and between groups of residents, tourists, managers and politicians concerning the capacity elements. A forum for regulation, coordination and compromise is necessary. Clearly carrying capacity management needs to be based on detailed policies and management objectives which specify what action can be taken to bring excess capacity issues into balance.

Finally, if capacity could be calculated and its impending arrival recognised, this would lead to further difficult questions as to what is to be done next. How willing and able are decision makers to manage the impacts and their underlying causes? In this field of multiple, uncoordinated agencies, there can be a major mismatch between policy intentions and actual outcome. *Implementation of visitor management policies is often the major stumbling block.* Of course, more tourists do not necessarily lead to more problems, or to greater negative impacts. Policies, goals and effective action could help mitigate capacity problems. Evidence from current research suggests that probably this most crucial element of carrying capacity, the capacity to get things done and put policy into action is the most elusive of all. In simple terms, the tourism industry is invariably uncoordinated, between levels, sectors (public and private) and for particular locations, such as heritage cities. The suggestion that tourism would become more sustainable through pro-active management if only the carrying capacity of destinations were known, is a fallacy. Carrying capacity is complex, and tourism managers will need to take a more comprehensive approach if this concept is to have any positive role in tourism management. The key difficulty remains one of incorporating value judgements of capacity attributes into the decision making process, with management objectives and capacity indicators set beforehand, rather than pursuing some all encompassing mythical value. Subsequent chapters will show that the wider understanding of capacity, in both the public and private sectors, is virtually non-existent, save for a few limited examples.

5 Europe-wide survey of visitor impacts and management responses

5.1 Introduction

The previous chapter has revealed the complexities of the concept of carrying capacity. Its application in practice is further complicated by the paucity of accurate data readily available to tourist agencies at most levels of management. The data which does exist tends to be based primarily on the more quantifiable economic aspects, often derived from national sources or simple *ad hoc* estimates. Little, if any, data is ever collected systematically in tourist destinations, and what is tends to be limited to simple visitor counts, accommodation surveys, or the restricted analysis of local market sector studies. Thus, while in theory, the concept of capacity seems rather logical and appealing, its implementation has provided a major stumbling block to the practical application of effective visitor management.

The purpose of this chapter is to explore this conflict between data availability and management strategies in European historic towns and cities. Based on a postal survey of local tourist organisations throughout the Continent, a questionnaire was used to examine the problems associated with tourism activity in different locations, and to identify what, if anything, had been done to mitigate the problems through visitor management.

5.2 Survey methodology

Most towns and cities in Europe have local tourist boards. Often these tend to be the agencies charged with responsibility for tourist promotion, providing information services and industry guidance in their respective communities. In this context, a survey of Local Tourist Board Directors was conducted to explore how communities in European historic towns and cities are responding to ever increasing visitor numbers, and what impact tourism is having on their cultural heritage. Key objectives of the survey were to determine as far as possible what local tourist boards knew about their local industry; what, if any, problems were perceived; and what actions were being taken to address these problems. An additional objective was to identify prospective case-study communities, showing good knowledge of tourism activity and pro-active management activity, for possible inclusion in a more detailed study later in the project.

A general set of guidelines were drawn up to determine which historic towns and cities were to be included in the survey:

1. *The town/city should not have more than 300,000 people or less than 20,000.* This population level was chosen because the original study was designed to examine capacity management issues within town and city settings. It was decided that much smaller towns or villages would be more likely to represent tourist sites, rather than dual-use settings. In contrast, it was felt that much larger cities would absorb the tourist function much more readily, with many impacts on cultural heritage derived from numerous sources apart from tourist activity. If at all possible, capital cities were also excluded from the project as their 'tourist draw' is often affected by socio-political interest in addition to cultural heritage, which would be difficult to compare with smaller heritage towns and cities;

2. *The town should be renowned for its historic attractions and cultural heritage.* It has been suggested that tourism activity is shifting away from simple beach/recreation based holidays in Europe to take on a more cultural flavour. Historic towns and cities are becoming popular destinations not only for 'weekend breaks', but increasingly as part of multi-centre excursions around countries and the continent. Thus towns and cities with famous monuments, the location of historic events, or unique cultural settings, not designed with the tourist in mind, are coming under increasing visitor pressure;

3. *The town should represent a popular or emerging tourist destination.* In order to examine capacity issues it was necessary to study destinations that may be having 'capacity' problems. Although there are numerous towns and cities of cultural heritage in Europe, not all represent tourist destinations. Many have one or two interesting monuments, or may have had some significant historic event which took place within their boundaries, but these

do not always represent enough of an attraction to draw in significant numbers of visitors to create management problems; and,

4. *The town or city might be known for its visitor management methods.* This study of 'capacity management' was also looking for elements of good practise alongside the identification of 'capacity issues'. As such, towns and cities of cultural heritage that had also managed to limit the negative effects of tourism were considered to be important for comparative analysis of transferable techniques.

Based on these general criteria an initial register of possible destinations was established. Lists of potential study towns and cities were drawn up for each European country, and sent to their National Tourist Office (NTO) representative in Great Britain. Each country's NTO was invited to examine the list, and to advise on the destinations being included in the study, against a brief outline of the project's objectives. In addition, NTOs were asked to provide the names of, and addresses for, the Directors of each local tourist board in the destinations specified. Through this process, 27 countries, including Austria, Belgium, Bulgaria, the Czech Republic, Denmark, Estonia, Finland, France, Germany, Gibraltar, Greece, Hungary, Ireland, Italy, Luxembourg, Malta, the Netherlands, Norway, Poland, Portugal, Roumania, Slovenia, Spain, Sweden, Switzerland, Turkey, and the United Kingdom, were included in the preliminary stages of this research.

Following adjustment of the initial list, based on recommendations from the National Tourist Organisations, a group of 165 towns and cities were selected for inclusion in the study and sent an invitation to participate in the research. Copies of the four-page questionnaire *(Appendix 1)*, cover-letter, and pre-addressed return envelope were delivered in early June, 1993. A 'reminder notice' (including questionnaire and envelope) were sent approximately one month later to non-respondents. Two months after the initial posting, 114 completed forms had been received along with three 'letters of reply', representing an overall response of 71 percent, from 20 different countries.

Wherever possible, cover-letters were addressed to the Director, as specific individuals, of local tourist boards, and in most cases, were translated into the official language of the country in question. The questionnaire itself, however, was only produced in English primarily for two reasons. First, although the use of industry jargon was avoided when at all possible, it was still considered probable that some terminology would have proven difficult to translate. Thus to try and avoid as much discrepancy with interpretation, English was used for all participants. Although the ability of each participant to respond in English raised a similar issue, it was considered probable that at least one member of the tourist board in these significant European destinations would be able to help with question interpretation and response. Second, and equally important, logistical reasons made it necessary to use English text only. As the translation of the cover-letters proved, some European languages tend to have longer words or phrases to convey the English equivalent. Since the formal lay-out of the original English text left little room for adjustment in question length and response, it was not possible to translate the full questionnaire in the space allowed without omitting some questions.

Figure 5.1 shows the locations of the towns and cities which participated in the project. Not all of these destinations necessarily conform to all of the criteria noted for inclusion in the study. In some, tourism activity may not have been excessive; in others the current population exceeded or fell-short of the initial parameters. However, in all cases, these communities were representative of the country's cultural heritage, and could be considered as popular or emerging tourist destinations. The next section provides a series of descriptive and nominal statistics on the respondent towns and cities, as a basis for analysis and interpretation of the more ordinal data on impacts and management issues which follows in section 5.4.

5.3 The respondents

The resident populations of responding towns and cities ranged quite significantly at the extremes, from a low of 1,800 estimated for Delphi, Greece, to the high of 800,000 indicated by Wroclaw, Poland. However, only about 10 percent of all destinations were below the 20,000 mark, with a similar percent exceeding the 300,000 level. The remainder (approximately 80 percent) fell within the pre-determined range, with a majority having between 50,000 and 200,000 residents and representing small to medium sized towns and cities.

Most destinations surveyed had some difficulty in providing empirical evidence of actual visitor counts, behavioral patterns or different activities pursued by their tourist markets. Although when asked to indicate the current volume of tourists, most (80 percent) did offer a figure, a significant minority suggested the numbers they gave were purely conjectural. Estimated levels of visitors varied enormously. Some respondents noted relatively low visitor counts, such as Braga (Portugal) with only 10,000 per annum; others recorded extremely high visitor counts of many millions, such as Edinburgh (Scotland) with 12,800,000, and Venice (Italy) with 10,000,000 visitors per annum. The average volume of visitor traffic to the respondent communities is estimated at 2,000,000 per annum. Figure 5.2 shows the spread of visitor numbers over the spectrum of response.

Figure 5.1 Location of participating towns and cities

In terms of visitor numbers on the busiest 'tourist' days of the year, less than half of the participants were willing or able to give a response. Of those who did, levels ranged from lows of under 500, to highs of over 300,000 visitors. Ten percent suggested that the most visitors they had on any one day was under 5,000, similarly another ten percent estimated this level at between 5,000 and 15,000. The vast majority estimated their peak day volume at between 15,000 and 85,000. Three cities (Czetochowa, Poland; Rostock, Germany; and Rimini, Italy) put their 'busiest day' estimate at over 200,000 visitors. Obviously some caution must be used in the evaluation of these particular figures. It is likely that while the question was meant to determine what were the peak visitor flows on the busiest day of the year, the question may have been interpreted as the combined total of 'busy days'.

Figure 5.2 Annual visitor numbers

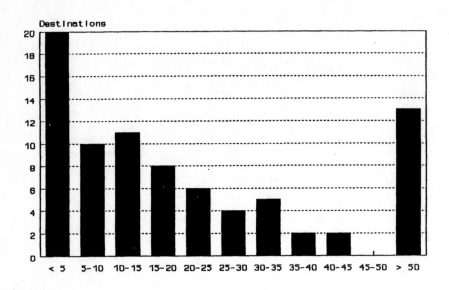

Overall, the majority of the historic towns and cities participating in this study were day visitor centres. In most cases, excursionists were noted to account for 65-85 percent of all visitors: the average length of stay was suggested as 5.5 hours, with a relatively normal distribution, ranging from a

70

low of 1.3, to a high of 12 hours a day. Overnight tourists, representing up to one-third of all visitors, were estimated to stay an average of 1.9 nights, ranging from 1 to 10 nights, but highly skewed around the average. As might be expected, peak visitor months corresponded with the European summer season of June, July and August. In addition, about three-quarters of the respondents also indicated the months of April, May, September and October as significant in terms of visitor numbers, with several noting the staging of particular festivals or other relevant holiday events. In all cases, however, a significant minority of respondents was unable to give accurate figures on lengths of stay, visitor numbers, or the proportion of overnight tourists to excursionists, and many who did indicated that the values were purely their best estimate.

As might be expected with historic destinations, the key reason for visiting the different communities, noted by one-half of the respondents, was the 'historic town centre', with a further one-quarter suggesting a specific site or attraction. Secondary reasons included the opportunity for shopping, and for business purposes. Tertiary reasons were given as the pursuit of a variety of leisure based activities such as attending plays and concerts, shopping, sporting activities and educational purposes. The main attractions in most destinations, were noted as cathedrals or other religious buildings, and castles or fortified town walls. Key secondary attractions were primarily local museums, or specific monuments, often in the historic centre of the community.

An interesting observation about this data set is the link that can be made between those destinations noting a high proportion of visitors to a single site (e.g. the Cathedral in Chartres (France), or Kronborg Castle in Helsingor (Denmark)) and those communities where tourists tend to visit the whole town centre (e.g. Oxford (UK) or Bruges (Belgium)). Destinations with a prominent attraction seemed better able or willing to offer an estimate of their visitor flows, perhaps because of the predominance of these 'single' sites or attractions. Overall, visitor volumes at specific sites ranged from lows of a few thousand such as the Bear Pits in Berne (Switzerland), to highs of 2.5 million at Canterbury Cathedral (UK), 3.5 million at Heidelberg Castle (Germany) and 5.5 million at Lourdes (France). However, only one-third of all respondents noted that visitor counts at specific sites were actually measured, and these tended to represent attractions charging an entrance fee. In addition, although most destinations did offer annual estimates of visitor numbers at key attractions, they were not able to identify the maximum capacity of the site, or the daily average over the peak tourist season.

On the whole it would seem that most destinations have very little empirical evidence on which to base their observations at the local level. Only one-half of the communities surveyed had ever undertaken some form of local tourism study, and if they did, these were either parking/traffic surveys or market research/ economic impact studies. Only one-quarter of all respondents had ever commissioned physical or cultural impact studies, with virtually all research taking place since the beginning of the 1990s. It would seem, therefore, that the analysis of tourism and its effects on a destination are primarily based on random observation, visitor counts at individual sites, or the best possible estimate by local tourist boards based on an extrapolation from national or regionally collated data. With this in mind, the next section looks at the major effects of tourism in destinations as seen through the eyes of local tourist boards.

5.4 Major impacts and problems

It has often been implied that if the ratio of tourists to residents exceeds a certain value then problems may begin to emerge, culminating in an overt dislike of tourists and resident antagonism (e.g. Doxey, 1975). As noted in Chapter 3, key reasons for this intolerance are often derived from the 'crowding-out' of 'local' shops, being replaced by 'tourist' outlets; the 'crowding-out' of local infrastructure, such as public transport; the possible increase in petty crime such as 'pick-pocketing' and other personal theft; and the shift in the local economy towards a 'foreign' market while neglecting the needs of the resident community. In this survey, of those respondents who identified both a resident and transient (tourist) population, approximately one-half had a calculated 'host/guest' ratio of up to 10:1 (i.e. ten tourists for every resident). Beyond this level there were no identifiable concentrations or patterns in ratios, and in most cases this was estimated to be less than 50:1 at peak times. In a few exceptions, however, this value was somewhat higher such as Pisa (Italy) at 75:1; Helsingor (Denmark) at 90:1; Killarney (Ireland) at 110:1; and Venice (Italy) at 135:1. In two particular examples, the calculation represented extreme ratios with nearly 350:1 in Lourdes (France) and just over 600:1 for Delphi (Greece). These two extremes, however, are the result of a relatively small resident population (16,300 and 1,800 respectively), and are for locations which are in effect either a tourist 'site' (Delphi), or an international destination of pilgrimage (Lourdes). In all cases, these ratios were based on calculations derived from destination visitor estimates compared to population census data provided by the respondents and must therefore be viewed with some caution, in light of the lack of empirical evidence to support visitor estimates.

To better understand the impact of tourism in the responding destinations, a series of statements were posed which highlighted the problems often associated with the high host/guest ratios noted above. Respondents were asked to indicate their level of agreement[1] with the statement as it related to their community. On the whole, most respondents disagreed with statements which suggested that a particular element of the capacity network, described in the previous chapter, had been exceeded. Over two-thirds of respondents *agreed* that most local business served a tourist market either directly or indirectly, and over 50 percent *agreed* that most local business would object to attempts being made to reduce visitor numbers in the destination. In contrast, the possible consequence of resident intolerance, or the desire to have fewer tourists in their towns was not considered to be an issue (70 percent and 67 percent disagree respectively). Overall, the most strongly rejected statement (74 percent disagree) concerned the rise in personal violence corresponding with greater tourist numbers. A summary of these responses is shown in Figure 5.3. All of these statements were examined in relation to the independent variables noted above (i.e. host/guest ratios; population levels; and tourist volume). Surprisingly, no evident or clear relationship could be established between any of these variables and the opinions expressed by the local tourist boards. For example, when a destination noted a very high host/guest ratio, this did not necessarily correspond with an agreement of resident intolerance, or the trend towards a local tourism-based economy.

A similar set of statements, but approaching this topic from a slightly different perspective, asked respondents to indicate whether, and to what extent, certain issues were considered to be problems in their communities. As the response to the previous set of statements revealed, most local tourist boards did not see any problems created by tourism development or activity in their towns and cities. One key exception, however, concerned traffic related issues. Car parking, traffic congestion and tourist coach parking were mentioned by over three-quarters of all respondents, who noted these to be minor problems at the very least. In contrast, tourist crowding in local shops and people congestion in city streets were not considered to be problems. Not surprisingly, car and coach parking were significant issues for the majority of these historic towns and cities. However, while traffic congestion was significant, the effects on local air quality, or its contribution to resident dislike of tourists, were not considered of further consequence. Other problems acknowledged, but not to the same extreme or at the same frequency, included the lack of attractions to keep tourists longer, and the erosion or accidental damage of historic sites. A summary of these findings is presented in Figure

---

[1] A seven point scale ranging from *Strongly Agree* to *Strongly Disagree* was used. In the following analysis, **Agree** refers to the sum of responses indicating *Strongly Agree, Agree* and *Mildly Agree*. **Disagree** refers to the sum of responses indicating *Strongly Disagree, Disagree*, and *Mildly Disagree*.

Figure 5.3 Tourism impacts and consequences

Statement	Percent AGREE	Percent NEUTRAL	Percent DIS-AGREE
Most businesses in our town/city serve a tourist market either directly or indirectly	70	12	18
Most businesses would object to measures to reduce tourist numbers in the town/city	59	15	26
Local rents have increased in the town/ city because of tourism development	30	15	55
The average spend per tourist has decreased as tourist numbers have increased	29	21	50
Theft has increased with greater tourist numbers	28	17	55
Many local residents would like fewer tourists to visit the town/city	19	14	67
Local residents are becoming less tolerant of tourists in the town/city	18	12	70
Since tourism development there are fewer shops directly serving local daily needs	11	11	78
Traditional arts and crafts have been replaced by lower quality products for tourists	10	18	72
Personal violence has increased with greater tourist numbers	7	19	74

Figure 5.4 Potential problems of tourism

	Major problem	Problematic	Minor problem	Not a problem	Don't know
Car parking	18	44	23	14	1
Tourist coach parking	16	38	24	21	1
Traffic congestion	15	31	29	24	1
Lack of attractions to keep tourists longer	14	22	27	35	2
Crowded pedestrian spaces	3	9	24	63	1
Local air quality	2	10	20	65	3
Erosion/ accidental damage to sites	1	15	37	43	4
Crowded local shops	1	6	22	70	1
Local resident dislike of tourism	1	6	21	69	3
Vandalism by tourists	0	4	27	65	4

5.4. These findings were also compared to various independent variables from the data set. As before, no significant relationship could be established between host/guest ratios, tourism numbers and population levels, and the problem outcomes.

Another measure of capacity related issues can be derived from visitor satisfaction levels. One way of examining this is through the analysis of tourist complaints. As such, respondents were asked to indicate the volume of complaints they received from tourists on a variety of issues. Very few destinations, however, indicated that they ever received complaints to suggest that 'visitor capacity' was a local issue. Although problems were noted with parking by over two-thirds of the destinations, and the provision of accommodation by just under one-half, these complaints were primarily received on a monthly basis. Only a very few destinations indicated that they ever received complaints on either a daily or weekly basis. As with the previous two sets of data, there was no clear relationship between the recorded levels of tourists' complaints, and the levels of visitors in the different towns or cities. A summary of these results is presented in Figure 5.5.

Figure 5.5 Tourists' complaints

Complaint	Daily	Weekly	Monthly	Not at all	Don't Know
Can't park	9	17	34	34	6
Town congested with traffic	9	12	19	54	6
Can't find TIC	3	11	21	60	5
Not enough/ too expensive accommodation	2	17	29	46	6
Streets/ sites overcrowded	2	5	10	77	6
Have to wait in-line to see attractions	1	5	2	86	6
Entrance fees too high	1	3	14	77	5
Nowhere to eat/ not enough restaurants	0	4	5	85	6

Clearly the results of this exercise can only be taken as indicative of the problems which historic towns and cities are faced with as a result of tourism development and activity. Not all local tourist boards are in a position to receive complaints, or keep a record of this activity. In addition, many tourists may simply not take the effort to complain, particularly if a return visit to that destination is unlikely in the near future, and/or there are language problems in making the complaint. Equally significant, local tourist boards may have been unwilling to admit to problems, or perhaps are ignorant of the negative impacts of tourism and how they can translate into issues and 'complaints'. In addition, it is possible that this level of self-criticism may be too exacting, given that respondents are supporting and encouraging an industry which may be having an adverse effect on either the resident or tourist populations, or both. With this in mind, it may be possible that the acknowledgement of traffic related problems are more a reflection of their own responsibilities, rather than a sign that these are the only important issues of concern or problems with tourism. Local tourist boards generally have little influence over traffic planning and management (and historic towns were not designed with the car or coach in mind) so these problems cannot be laid at their door, and it is therefore easier to acknowledge them.

A series of comparative cross-tabulations was undertaken to better understand the responses, and to relate various tourism impacts, acknowledged problems and visitor complaints. For example, a comparison was made between those respondents who tended to agree that 'many local residents would like fewer tourists to visit the town/city' and the acknowledged problem of a 'local resident dislike of tourism'. Whilst 20 percent of respondents believed that local residents would like fewer tourists to come to the destination, only one-half of these suggested that 'local resident dislike of tourism' was a problem. In another comparison, it was found that although 30 percent noted a resident dislike of tourists, only one-half of this number believed (or acknowledged?) that local residents were becoming less tolerant of visitors. There may be several explanations of such limited only correlations, including a lack of local awareness of the impacts of tourism on the resident population.

A second set of comparisons was made between those issues which were noted as being problems for the destinations, such as parking and traffic congestion, and the recorded level of tourist complaints on the subjects. In these examples there was a closer correlation of responses. Three-quarters of respondents noted traffic congestion as a problem and just under one-half also indicated that tourists tended to complain about this issue. Similarly, 85 percent of respondents suggested that car parking was a local problem, and two-thirds noted this was a tourist complaint as well. However, despite what appears to be an element of 'traffic awareness' by local tourist boards, there appears to be relatively little understanding of visitor transport patterns, or the proportion of traffic created by tourist visits. About one-third of respondents only were willing or able to estimate what proportion of local traffic was generated by tourists. Estimates ranged from a low of one percent to a high of ninety-five percent, with clusters around ten to fifteen percent, and fifty to eighty percent. In addition, although the private motor-car was considered to be the most popular mode of transport for tourists to most destinations (followed by the tour coach, and train respectively), only seventy-five percent were able or prepared to estimate what proportion of their tourist market arrived by these different transport modes. Such responses suggest that although traffic problems associated with tourism are clearly acknowledged, they are only partially understood.

5.5 Visitor management responses

The final element of the survey was designed to see what, if any, actions were being taken by local tourist boards in terms of tourism management, such as having a tourism strategy or development plan. Just under two-thirds of all destinations stated they had a tourism strategy, of which eighty percent had a city level plan. Of the remainder, respondents indicated that their strategies were guided by a higher level regional or national level plan. The most common primary objective of these tourism strategies was to increase visitor numbers. Extending the visitors' stay; encouraging tourism outside the peak season; and better management of current numbers were also commonly noted. All, except for the better management of tourism, however, are essentially growth related objectives, aimed at increasing the overall level of tourism.

Based on the analysis of tourism issues and problems in the previous section, it is not necessarily surprising that the prime objectives of local tourism strategies have not been to reduce the negative impacts of the industry. In fact, based on an assessment of key objectives, it would seem that most strategies do not appear to have many management objectives at all. The reduction of tourism's negative impacts, the spreading of benefits to more local people, or the better coordination of local agencies and businesses involved in tourism were only mentioned by relatively few, and as secondary or tertiary objectives. Only one destination indicated that its key strategy objective was to reduce tourist numbers, but at the same time, it also wanted to increase spending, encourage visitors to come outside the peak season, and strongly agreed that most local business served a tourist market.

There was no general pattern in the data to suggest that as tourist volume increased then a destination would be more likely to have a tourism strategy. Similarly, as the ratio of tourists to residents increased, the presence or absence of a tourism plan did not necessarily correspond. For example, while one-half of those having tourism strategies had a host/guest of 30:1 or less, ten percent of respondents with an estimated ratio of greater than 70:1 did not have tourism strategies. On the whole, there was no clear relationship between the objectives of a destination's tourism strategy and any of the independent variables discussed earlier. As tourist numbers, or ratios increased, key objectives of some strategies were still to increase visitor numbers, or increase the tourist season. As with the recognition of tourism problems, strategy objectives would appear to be based on the more quantifiable aspects of tourism economics, and not on a wider range of capacity elements. Figure 5.6 summarizes the key objectives of destination tourism strategies as identified by the local tourist boards.

Figure 5.6 Summary of strategy objectives

	First objective	Second objective	Third objective
Increase current visitor numbers	28	5	10
Encourage visitors to come outside the peak season	11	17	13
Extend the stay of current visitors	10	12	13
Better manage current visitors	10	11	4
Increase spending per visitor	7	12	6
Decrease negative impacts	4	6	3
Spread economic benefits to more local people	1	1	8
Reduce current visitor numbers	1	0	1
Spread visitors throughout the town/city	0	5	6
Better co-ordinate local agencies involved in tourism	0	3	6

(Column totals do not add to 100 percent because not all respondents had tourism strategies, nor did all indicate three objectives for their strategy)

A series of comparisons was made between the stated objectives of the local tourism strategies, and the level of agreement or disagreement with the statements concerning impacts and problems listed in Figures 5.3 and 5.4. Based on the previous analysis, it was not surprising to find relatively little connection between the recognition of issues and problems often associated with tourism, and corresponding corrective management objectives in the tourism strategy. In one example where resident dislike of tourism was considered to be a major problem, the primary objective of the tourism strategy was still to increase visitor numbers. In other examples, where respondents agreed that local residents would prefer a reduction in visitor numbers, this was not reflected in the primary objectives of the tourism strategy, which again were to increase visitor numbers. Similar conflicts between problems and objectives were evident for parking and traffic congestion. Even when current visitors were thought to arrive by car and tourist coach, with traffic congestion and parking acknowledged as major problems, the key objective of many strategies was still to increase tourist numbers.

At first glance it would seem that neither industry management nor the recognition of non-economic negative impacts are considered as serious issues by most local tourist boards, or they know very little about these problems and thus do nothing to understand or address them. Thus the assumption made earlier that local tourist boards might be responsible for local industry management, or have a significant influence over the rate of tourism development, appears to be largely erroneous. The vast majority (57 percent) of respondents indicated they were agencies of local or regional government, with responsibility for tourist promotion and information services. The remainder were either organisations sponsored by joint public/private sector initiatives (20 percent) or solely industry based. Again, responsibility tended towards tourist promotion and co-ordination of information and interpretative services in the destination. However, it may be that even if some local tourist boards were cognisant of these issues, they may not be in a position to take action even if they so desired. What actions have been taken to combat these issues are discussed below, including the application of a tourist tax; differential pricing at attractions; the provision of tourist information and signposting, and traffic management options.

One principle of resource management is that the user or polluter should pay for their consumption or modification of the resource. In tourism, very often what is consumed as the product is the cultural and natural heritage of a destination, commonly as a public good. Such consumption does not tend to show up in the 'tourism accounts' of industry operators, tourists or even the destination as a whole. One way of confronting this 'cost' is through the

80

application of some form of 'tourist tax', which passes a portion of these 'operating costs' on to the consumer. In this survey, 26 percent of respondents indicated that they operated a specific tourist tax, ranging from a bed-tax in hotels, parking fees for tour coaches, and a meal tax in restaurants. The bed-tax was the most common form of getting tourists to pay more for the use of the destination (used by nearly all who operated a tourist tax). However, this indicates that it is generally the overnight visitor, representing on average, less than one-quarter of the tourist population in this survey, who pays the highest price.

Another method of passing on the cost of using resources is to charge an entrance fee or request donations from those visiting a site. This is a common approach, particularly in the private sector, but when public sector agencies begin to place admission charges on what were once 'free' public goods, less than charitable feelings amongst local residents may begin to emerge. Given that local hospitality is a key element of the tourism product, it is necessary to find some way of 'repaying' or spreading the benefits to the community. A well tried approach is to offer special reductions or 'free entry' to residents where they wish to visit or use local facilities and attractions. However, in this survey while one-half of respondents indicated that their key local attractions did charge admissions fess, only ten percent offered a resident reduction. As the key objective of the tourism plans indicates, this type of spreading of tourism benefits does not appear to be a priority for most local tourism agencies or attractions.

A third and common approach to limiting negative tourism impacts and contributing to visitor management is through the provision of tourist literature and information services. This helps the tourist to acquaint themselves with a destination, and begins to interpret the environment they are visiting. If well prepared, tourist literature not only tells the visitor what the destination has to offer, and where to find various attractions, but it can also be used to influence visitor behaviour and encourage 'environmental' responsibility. However, if this aspect of tourist information is to be successful then it needs to be readily available for all tourists in terms of the right location, the right cost, and in a form usable by all. In this survey, most destinations did provide a basic tourist information service. In all but one, each destination operated a central tourist information centre and the majority supplied tourist maps free-of-charge at least in the national language of the destination. Several towns and cities also supplied tourist literature in other European languages, but these were less 'freely' available (e.g. the native language brochure was free but the translations were available for a fee). The most common European languages used in brochures included English, German, French, Dutch, Spanish and Italian. Depending on the location of the town or city, other 'regional' languages were also utilized (e.g. Scandinavian and Eastern European languages). In several cases the multi-language publications appeared as one brochure or booklet with all languages included. Some destinations also included brochures in Russian and Japanese. A summary of this information is listed in Figure 5.7.

A fourth and final element of managing tourism impacts which was examined in this survey concerned aspects of traffic management. As car parking, traffic congestion, and tourist coach parking were considered to be likely problems for historic towns and cities, it seemed probable that these destinations would implement some measures to mitigate these problems.

Figure 5.7 Provision of tourist information

	Percent YES	Percent NO
Central TIC	99	1
Tourist signposting	83	17
Tourist maps at transport nodes	81	19
Free maps	81	19
Free maps in multiple languages	73	27
Interpretation panels	55	45

Measures to influence traffic were common management activities, and despite the lack of knowledge displayed in this survey concerning traffic related issues, the majority of destinations operated a variety of traffic schemes. The most commonly cited was the provision of a shuttle-bus service for tourists from either the tour-coach park or the train station. Other common options included a coach drop-off/pick-up point somewhere in or near the historic centre of the destination, and the use of designated coach parks for visiting tour buses. Perhaps in response to traffic levels in historic towns, virtually all survey respondents indicated that they operated some form of town centre pedestrianisation scheme. In most cases this was generally one or two key shopping streets in the city centre and in some cases was only operational during the peak tourist season. Just under two-thirds of respondents did note that they also operated a 'park and ride' scheme, but it would seem from further investigation and subsequent discussions that what was actually meant by this term was often misunderstood by participants. A summary of response to these questions is given in Figure 5.8.

Figure 5.8 Traffic management measures

	Percent YES	Percent NO
Pedestrianisation of town centre (or part of it)	88	12
Shuttle bus from coach park/train station	84	16
Coach drop-off point	75	25
Coach parks	74	26
Park and Ride	62	38
Residents pay lower public transport charges	2	98

5.6 Conclusions

The purposes of this questionnaire survey were to examine the prevalence of capacity issues in Europe's historic towns and cities, and to review management responses to such issues. However, as the findings of this chapter suggest, there are a number of significant issues which need to be addressed before the application of carrying capacity could ever become an effective reality.

Capacity issues A fundamental conclusion drawn from the survey is that most tourist destinations would appear to know relatively little about their visitors: their numbers, where they come from, what they do, or how long they stay in the location. Perhaps partly as a consequence of this most local tourist boards in European historic towns and cities do not consider they have capacity problems which require management actions. Although this finding may be partly a result of the survey method, or the primarily promotional function of the tourist board respondents, the consistency in response is significant.

As the survey suggests, when there is a recognition of tourist problems, these tend to be physical constraints or economic issues, and not based on a full analysis of the industry. As has been discussed in the previous chapter, capacity is a function of six elements, but in most destinations it would appear that only two or three are considered. This is perhaps indicative of the justification behind tourism development and the rationale for the existence of most tourist boards. Tourism is generally promoted because of its economic potential in job creation and foreign exchange. Notwithstanding the benefits of enhanced understanding through tourism, invariably the industry is not developed for its contribution to international harmony and the more perceptual elements of capacity are not a primary concern. Indeed, the 'community' and 'visitor' elements were rarely recognised or acknowledged.

Some 'economic' and especially 'physical' constraints were more evident, and a recurrent theme in the study was the issue of traffic problems. Although this can be a direct result of increased tourism activity, especially in places with a high concentrations of day-visitors, it must also be recognised that historic towns, originally developed before the advent of the internal combustion engine, are liable to have conflicts with modern methods of transportation. This then becomes a more general issue in a changing society, and the contribution of tourism to this problem needs to be viewed in the appropriate context, alongside other modern transport issues. Despite the recognition of traffic impacts, it would appear that very few destinations actually have any hard evidence to suggest that tourist related activities are the key instigator of such impacts. The lack of empirical data appears to be widespread in European historic towns and cities, and this presents further problems for tourism management.

Capacity management If destinations do not fully understand the local tourism industry, how can they hope to appreciate capacity issues and effectively respond with management objectives and actions? As the response to basic factual questions suggests, there appears to be a general lack of empirical evidence behind the development and application of tourism strategies. This presents a particular problem for tourism capacity management, for this means that management activity cannot address the negative effects of tourism as the magnitude and dimensions of the industry are not fully understood. As a result, many destinations seem to be following a growth or development policy, both spatially and temporally, but without setting up indicators to warn them of impending problems. Management of tourism in relation to capacity considerations is dependent on a fuller understanding of the industry and its

84

impacts than would generally seem to be the case at present. There appears to be a serious shortcoming in knowledge at the local level, which can only be rectified through detailed and comprehensive analysis of the industry in each location. However, the results of this survey must be viewed with some caution. While in many destinations, local tourist boards represent the 'public face' of tourism management, they often have a promotional focus. Actual development policies, planning strategies and transport management invariably reside with other local government personnel in land-use planning, engineering and economic development departments. While this does not negate the validity of the response, it does offer some insight as to why some problems and constraints of the industry are not readily recognised or acknowledged. A lack of integration of the various components of the industry can result in a lack of an integrated response to capacity issues and capacity management. However, as the next chapter shows, there are some notable exceptions of destinations which have taken significant steps to better understand their local tourism industry, to integrate industry elements, and to improve their approach to visitor management.

6 Case studies

6.1 Introduction

In order to develop current evidence from local representatives, the project team selected a group of towns and cities to be included in a workshop discussion of current visitor pressures and management responses. In preparation, a further examination of Chester, an English cathedral city, and Heidelberg, a German university city, both with current initiatives in proactive visitor management, were also considered.

The provincial centres included in this chapter are national, and to various degrees, international, places of cultural pilgrimage. Focused on a cathedral, Chartres, has obvious physical parallels with Chester, and especially Canterbury, whilst Heidelberg and Coimbra share historic places of learning with Oxford. Helsingor illustrates both the defensive and dockyard inheritance evident in Venice, together with the vagaries of literary association, whilst Bruges is representative of the civic tradition manifested so strongly in the Low Countries.

The discussion below focuses on a few of the specific issues raised by each town and the responses initiated. To various degrees, each town or city shows three essential pre-requisites for effective and beneficial visitor management, viz:

. an individual, or group, with strong personal commitment to both the heritage, and the presentation of the place;

. a willingness to network between public, private and non-governmental organisations, offices and groups in new configurations in order to meet new challenges; and

. a growing consistency in the development of short, and medium-term, surveys and plans which regularly inform the development and management processes.

6.2   Chartres

Chartres (42,000 population, 1991) is seen by most observers as a town dominated by one monumental attraction, its cathedral. Fronting the town's promotional pamphlet is Emile Male's statement, 'there is nothing that can compare with Chartres. Chartres is the very mind of the Middle Ages in visible form.' This 'mind' is exhibited, not only in the UNESCO World Heritage listed cathedral, but also in the churches, public buildings, early houses and historic districts of the town, as well as in five museums.

But for the majority of the estimated one million visitors a year, the visit focuses on the cathedral, and the town provides a key example of the problems associated with a well located centre, seen as a brief stop off on a chain of attractions which might include Paris (only 56 miles distant and 50 minutes by rail), Versailles and the Loire Valley. The town's representative, who introduced evidence from a sequence of recent surveys, regretted that 'visitors were just looking rather than visiting' and in doing so, raised an important question with regard to the quality of interaction between visitors and the heritage attraction. The cathedral and adjacent area of Chartres exhibit typical problems of rapid visit turnaround, parking, groups gathering, pressure on adjacent facilities and erosion of the heritage structure. Chartres attracts largely day visitors who are increasingly uninformed as to the historical and architectural qualities which they are invited to observe.

The need to interpret the mind of the Middle Ages through the cathedral and its surroundings became evident from a detailed survey of visitors undertaken in 1991. Wide ranging and innovative, it led to proposals for adding value to the visitor experience, conserving the historic context, and maintaining economic benefit. Proposals included a substantial 'gateway' visitor centre, since titled the International Medieval Centre of Chartres, to be located adjacent to the cathedral. This is expected to provide an additional attraction, as well as the essential information on the building to enhance and guide the visit. In addition there are also proposals for the management of visitor traffic, the extension of visits through events, and association with educational, research and cultural activities. The developing proposals for Chartres may be seen as:

. safeguarding the heritage resource;

. supplementing the visitor experience by provision of essential interpretation;

. extending the visit and visitor spend through development of events and other attractions; and

. careful product marketing in order to attract specialist interests, including associated education and research.

Although design proposals for the Centre, keystone to Chartres programme of visitor management, have been prepared, the scheme has yet to receive the local and national finance which are required. Whilst a range of initiatives to protect monuments, extend visitor range and enhance experiences are possible supported by visitor income, any effective re-statement of Chartres' meaning to the contemporary visitor requires the type of substantial initiative and finance that was proposed, but which remains on paper. Whilst the cathedral is a State owned monument, and is marketed internationally as a jewel of French culture, its presentation in context remains a largely local responsibility. The mismatch between international image and local resourcing is not unique to Chartres.

6.3   Chester

Chester (116,000 population, 1991) is a Roman city which shows it origins in plan form. The central, heritage area, is surrounded by a well maintained medieval wall, within which are a wide range of museum and other attractions, as well as a dense pattern of traditional and recent retail outlets.

Since the early 19th century, Chester has been a visitor venue, and its physical fragility was recognised in the late 1960s by one of the first British government inspired heritage studies (Insall, 1968). The study stressed the important role of the circling wall as a distributor, and this has been used to advantage in successive, planned, local initiatives. These include concentration of bus and coach parking outside the walls, provision of a variety of bus links around the city, pedestrianisation of extensive public areas, establishment of a pioneer heritage centre and latterly, considerable attention to customer care.

In 1993 a further, substantial, study of the future of historic Chester was commissioned by central and local government and English Heritage. The study, *Chester - The Future of an Historic City* by the Building Design Partnership, was published in 1994 and is summarised by Roebuck (1994). The report seeks to develop a methodology for analysing environmental capacity and development issues facing historic towns and cities. It builds on an earlier phase of the study, *Environmental Capacity and Development in Historic Cities*, undertaken by Arup (1993). The methodology includes: a clarification of the critical environmental capacity of the city or town, identifying those natural and cultural resources that are considered irreplaceable; the identification of current or anticipated issues of concern or opportunity resulting from major pressures acting upon the critical environmental capital; the specification of indicators to be used to establish whether the pressures are increasing or easing; and capacity guidelines, specifying threshold limits on levels and types of activities. Figure 6.1 summarises the issues, and indicators of capacity.

In commenting on the report, Roebuck (1994) makes an important distinction which is evident in Chester's subsequent discussions, and which has implications for the present study:

Discussions through the English Historic Towns' Forum suggest that many planning authorities already approach the production of their development plans in terms of environmental capacity and have been doing so for the last 20 years, the difference being that they do not describe it as such.

However it is clear that although many authorities may identify with the concept, the assessment of the environmental capacity of a city or town is something quite different from the preparation of a development plan.

The key to environmental capacity is the continual monitoring of change and its impacts and effects on the critical environmental capital, otherwise it is to a large extent relatively limited in its usefulness. Environmental capacity is related solely to the physical attributes of a place and in that way it is relatively singleminded. Indeed, many of the issues raised are management issues, and cannot be addressed entirely as part of the development plan process.

Currently Chester is in the process of evaluating and commissioning a sequence of physical development plans which include tourism and the visitor experience as an integral element in the planning process, for as Harrison (1993) has noted in his detailed discussion of capacity in Chester, 'these five factors: good planning practice, structure and local plan, government and European policy, sustainability and perception, together now put capacity issues centre stage in the planning of historic towns and cities.'

The city is also a leader amongst the walled towns of Europe which are examining conservation and tourism issues on a cross cultural basis. Chester maintains its local reputation as a good shopping centre, and as a good place to live, despite the annual arrival of 1.5 million visitors. Observation and local discussion suggest the following positive implications from the town:

. well integrated publication, sign and promotional systems with information readily available, and emphasising the extent of possible attractions;
. design and management of a wide range of paths, waiting and resting areas;
. continual local concern for 'in keeping' heritage initiatives and the inclusion of new conservation projects in tourist routes;
. close relationship between land use planning, traffic management and tourist management processes; and

Figure 6.1   Examples of issues facing historic cities and possible indicators

ISSUES OF CONCERN OR OPPORTUNITY	INDICATORS
Impact of Tourism on Historic Core - wear and tear - pedestrian congestion - type of shops - parking problems (esp. coaches) - new uses for old buildings - wealth creation	• No. visitors • No. 'touristy' shops • Visitor enjoyment • Residents' frustration • Vacancy rate in city centre car parks • Traffic congestion • No. historic buildings in tourist use • Jobs attributable to tourism
Pedestrian-Vehicular Conflict in Historic Core - congestion - intimidation - delays - noise	• Accident rates • Pedestrian densities • Pedestrian comfort levels • Noise levels
Land Use Change in City Centre - pressure for office development - pressure for hotels - declining resident population - loss convenience shops - dead at night - loss garden areas - vacancy of upper floors	• No. residents • No. empty units • No. planning permissions • Traffic congestion • Rental levels • No. personal assaults at night
Damage to Listed Building Fabric - traffic emissions - vibration - tourist pressure - pressure for inappropriate conversions - lack of upkeep	• No. delisted • No. buildings at risk • Rental values • Traffic volume • NO_x measures • Amount of graffiti
Loss of Character and Setting of City - recent growth suburbs - infilling of green wedges - obstruction of skyline - poor approaches to city	• Distance to countryside from centre • Compactness (built area) • % open space to built area • Loss of viewlines • Residents' satisfaction • Rate of new development
Impact of tight Green Belt - town cramming - housing market distortion	• Loss of open space within city • Development land prices • House prices • Rate of new development

Source: Arup, 1993

. regular monitoring of visitor patterns on a detailed, urban design, scale and a willingness to respond to problems and opportunities.

The visitor programme for Chester is now pursued by means of the *Presenting Chester* partnership between public, private and voluntary sectors which has adopted a policy framework which ensures the advancement of the points above. This is being achieved through an extensive structure focused on a Standing Conference with working groups devoted to signing and traffic management; information and interpretation; resource development; and environmental improvement. These groups have identified over 50 projects which were then prioritised, with *The Chester Waterways Study* already completed. This is a strategic document, incorporating design guidelines to advance work by public and private sectors. Other priorities focus on a sequence of environmental improvement programmes, plans for interpretation, publication and education, improvements to tourist information facilities, and research into key traffic issues.

Chester's visitor presentation has long benefitted from local authority innovation, considered strategic planning, and a fundamental concern for customer care. It continues to provide a working laboratory for tourist management initiatives and has recently been party to a series of signal reports and proposals.

6.4   Canterbury

Canterbury is the premier cathedral city of England (41,250 population, 1991). Located between the Kent coast and London, it has long been a site of pilgrimage, and is particularly well placed to benefit, and suffer, from individual and group visits arriving on the South Coast, and from the Channel Tunnel. As a result the city has a very high visitor-to-host ratio (Page, 1992). There are many parallels between Chester and Canterbury, each serving as a market centre to its hinterland, each centred on a cathedral, each with a range of other significant tourist sites. In Canterbury, the Cathedral, St. Martin's Church and St. Augustine's Abbey are all World Heritage sites.

Canterbury was perhaps slower to develop its awareness of visitor impacts, although a traditional tourism study of 1975 revealed the very considerable impact on the local economy with some 2,500 full time jobs attributed to the industry. A further, parallel, study was undertaken in 1985 and recent figures suggest an annual visitor throughput of 2.25 million (Canterbury District Council, 1993). Until recently, however, tourism policies for Canterbury, though part of the physical and economic planning processes, have been broadscale, with reference to accommodation, length of stay and congestion rather than specific, place related, proposals. As in Oxford, tourism planning is a sensitive political issue with considerable public debate over investment, or programmes which would seem to favour visitors, rather than local residents.

The problems identified in Canterbury concern central area crowding (in an area only half a mile across), conflicts with traffic movements, over use of the Cathedral leading to identifiable physical damage, and apparent tourist ignorance of the range of opportunities available. The past few years have, however, seen a considerable increase in both the initiatives, and the personal energies, applied to visitor management in the city. Officers identify three factors as contributing to this positive role:

. recognition of the local Council's role as a catalyst for action by others;
. recognition that lateral thinking is needed to understand how the work of the various Council departments interlink, and how this influences what can be achieved; and
. recognition of the value of working in partnership with other groups. In particular, involving local businesses and making sure residents are part of the partnership brings support for what is to be achieved.

These factors are illustrated through integrated programmes in several key local authority areas.

The first concerns traffic and pedestrian management which includes a park and ride system for long term business parking, a voucher scheme for central area residents, the identification of new, effective, coach parking, and an emphasis on public transport, cycling and walking in future schemes. Carefully monitored pedestrianisation schemes have been effective in extending the tourist zone of the city.

The second, related, programme emphasises the development of trails and walkways which serve both residents and visitors, and involve positive urban design and landscape initiatives as well as signing and waymarking. The retail Longmarket, with its integral museum (English Historic Towns Forum, 1994) and the Riverside Walk project are indicative of the practical integration of traffic planning, tourism and leisure functions in the city, with a sequence of visitor trails also serving as effective pedestrian routeways between new car parks and city centre locations. The Riverside Walk project involves a high quality of design intervention, clear sign systems, and a marketing programme including trail leaflets.

A third issue being addressed involves the effective integration of such underused sites as St. Augustine's Abbey into the visitor's perception of opportunity. The need to extend tourist range, and to bring economic benefit to deserving sites requires substantial public investment, but is regarded as an essential long term goal.

Canterbury has stressed the programmed integration of fabric conservation, urban design, traffic management, visitor management and marketing. Its representatives note that, 'none of the measures we have been discussing are cheap, but we know that they work. In Canterbury we have been able to go a long way towards managing the impact of visitors effectively by a combination of practical measures, lateral thinking, partnerships and recognition of the City Council's role as a catalyst for action.'

In addition to the conclusions with regard to Chester above, we must therefore add the positive Canterbury implications:

. the crucial importance of new management configurations to meet new needs;

. the importance of seeing an historic centre and its visitors within a regional context;

. the necessity to capture the minds of a local population in recognising the economic benefits to be achieved from effective visitor management;

. the need for proactive and integrated proposals for town centre design which incorporate visitor needs.

These intentions have latterly been incorporated in the purpose of the Canterbury City Centre Initiative, a public/private sector company established as a three year experiment in 1994. This is intended to serve as a clearing house and co-ordinator for town centre initiatives, a focus for the implementation of the city's sustainable visitor management programme. It will have a strong monitoring and evaluation function, surveying tourist, retail and resident attitudes and behaviour and will initiate community based Tourism Workshops. It includes a schools' liaison project, together with a detailed programme of initiatives to ensure the sustainable basis of future tourism development.

The Canterbury and, to some degree, the Chester programmes represent considered local initiatives which have developed from recent British interest in the concept of High Street Management, and its extension to incorporate the concerns of city centre users. The influence of Canterbury, and other key members of the English Historic Towns Forum (Aldous, 1992) is evident in that organisation's recent policy document on visitor management, *Getting it Right* (English Historic Towns Forum, 1994).

6.5   Heidelberg

The City of Heidelberg (132,295 population, 1989) provides a fascinating example of a community response to visitor management. The approach currently being adopted is set out in *Guidelines on Tourism Heidelberg* (Heidelberg, 1993). It is estimated that this old university city has approximately 500,000 staying visitors, and 3.5 million day visitors per annum (1992 figures), placing the castle and the old town under particular pressure.

Located on the south bank of the Neckar, the core also contains the oldest university in Germany, with a student population of 27,000 and a wide range of specialist, internationally renowned institutes. Traditionally the visitor to Heidelberg has shared in the hillside and valley views to be attained from journeys beyond the city centre.

Precipitated by a range of publicised overcrowding issues, the guidelines have resulted from discussions between experts and citizens between June 1991 and June 1992. The topics of the ten public discussions are indicative of the breadth of this signal report: the new challenge of city tourism; streets and squares of Heidelberg, problems caused by street partying; tourism and traffic; what does Heidelberg's cultural life offer to tourists?; science and economy - possible locations; does Heidelberg need a new festival hall?; city marketing; the Heidelberg myth; Heidelberg and its districts; and is smooth tourism Utopia?

The resultant guidelines are seen as a commitment by the municipal authority, and a framework of reference for private industry. Their underlying principle is that whatever citizens, themselves, enjoy, tourists will also enjoy. Heidelberg is seeking to reorientate itself towards a socially acceptable, and environmentally friendly, style of tourism, with the qualitative aspects more important than the quantitative. The guidelines are structured around three dimensions, each with main and subsidiary objectives:

. Economic: securing present and future jobs in tourism on a seasonal and long term basis.

. Sociocultural: preserving the distinctive character of Heidelberg and promotion of the town's identity.

. Ecological: promoting an ecologically acceptable style of tourism.

In addition to the policy reorientation particular positive implications of the Heidelberg case are:

. re-targeting towards overnight tourism, and towards particular groups - including congress and university visitors, and those who can be attracted out of season, such as pensioners, students and young people;

. strategic shift towards seasonal working to capacity by transferring visitor potential into the low season;

. safeguarding of the identity and attraction of the city for local residents by, for example, providing a programme of cultural events, maintaining the 'resident's bonus' (ie keeping local hidden attractions off tourist trails and out of the guide books), and maintaining the local supply of essential everyday goods for locals in the Old Town, supported by municipal leases if necessary; and

. encouraging environmentally friendly travel by visitors to the town.

The community based development of shared intentions for tourism planning stands as a model for others to follow. It incorporates the majority of issues, and many of the favoured international solutions, found elsewhere in the present study. The success of Heidelberg's initiative will, of course, depend on a very wide range of co-ordinated individual actions. The concluding subscript to the plan must stand as a directive to future enquiry: 'Regular check on progress, examination and extension of the guidelines to continually establish agreement anew.'

6.6   Coimbra

Centrally located in Portugal, Coimbra (120,000 population, 1992) enjoys the riverside location, much pictured historic skyline and rich heritage that typify Iberian cities. In addition its reputation and publicity build expectation for the experience of an historic university, its human traditions and daily activities. Through the university and through song traditions, its image is hallowed by those who visit, and those who admire from afar. This epitomisation of Portugal has been further advanced through the presence of a leisure park, 'Portugal dos Pequenitos' which provides a model Portuguese experience for children.

Coimbra suffers from similar problems to those of Chartres, although in this case it is its popular identification as an 'Historic University Centre' which generates many of the issues of concentration and conflict. Both Chartres and Coimbra require a clarity of local authority vision which integrates visitor planning with the broader process of economic development and urban design. Both have nationally designated monuments which must be conserved and sustained through local initiative.

In Coimbra, particularly, the conflicts between various interested populations are evident. How, precisely, does the day visitor experience, or share in, the life of a University? Oxford provides one form of solution, with historic building visits and a specially designed attraction, but without such developed facilities, visitors and academics can be brought into unprofitable encounters. As with all the towns examined here, Coimbra has undertaken recent visitor surveys and, with limited resources, has initiated guided walk programmes and other forms of interpretation which serve both to manage visitor activity, and to enhance the visit.

Representatives emphasise the importance of a tourist plan which clearly relates visitor activity to evolving programmes of development and traffic management. It also seems essential to recognise the University as a very specific form of heritage attraction for which there is little consolidated international literature.

Currently Coimbra is undertaking a series of integrated initiatives to enhance visitor experiences and manage volumes and flows. These include promotion of Coimbra as a city within a wider region, welcome programmes which direct visitors, an upgrading of accommodation and services, the steady development of conference programmes appropriate to a university city, and the increased promotion of quality cultural events. Of special significance has been the development of two tour circuits, 'A Trip Through History' and 'A Trip Through Literature' available to visitor and education groups, and serving to extend visitor range with economic opportunities for those peripheral areas visited.

Fundamentally, it is the urban infrastructure which must respond to visitor, and resident, requirements. Priority is an upgrading of the fabric of the historic core, with a current renovation programme for some 20 percent, 300 properties, in the area. Coimbra's centre has recently been pedestrianised, with the incorporation of substantial new shopping opportunities. A strategy for much needed traffic management is now being pursued. Like many historic hill cities, traffic within the core raises particular problems which are to be resolved by the development of peripheral parking, and park and ride public transport to the centre. As elsewhere, both extensive public transport investment, and a change in driver attitudes, are required.

Coimbra has worked solidly to upgrade and integrate visitor facilities with the infrastructural changes which contemporary pressures place on an historic town. It sees increased visitor numbers (from the present 70,000 per annum), and longer stays, as essential to economic development, but already recognises the traffic, nightlife and other conflicts which can emerge.

The University remains both an opportunity and a key issue with regard to tourist development, raising problems which are, as yet, unresolved in the more experienced Oxford. Nationally renowned universities in ancient fabric attract visitors intent on a cultural experience, but too often offer an uneasy glimpse of an ancient institution defending itself again unwelcome attention. International organisations devoted to the management of historic, and of walled, towns exist but a regular international exchange with regard to the special problems of university cities in long overdue.

6.7   Helsingor

Helsingor (58,000 population, 1993), the Danish town to the north of Copenhagen in Jutland and home of Hamlet's castle, Kronborg, is an unlikely case study in this text. Helsingor was established in 1426 by a Charter of the Danish king, Erik of Pomerania, who introduced Sound Dues, a fee to be paid to the Danish Crown for ships passing through the narrows between Denmark and Sweden. Castles owned by the Danish Crown on either side of the Sound ensured that taxes were paid, and Helsingor, which was laid out by the king, attracted a wide range of foreign traders and advisers who were able to translate and negotiate with the various passing sea captains.

Today, Kronborg Castle is the town's major attraction, but rather like Warwick (UK), it is detached from the town and can be reached without experiencing the urban core. Whilst very useful for traffic management, this means that the castle, a national monument, is somewhat divorced from the town's planning process.

Inevitably, Helsingor grew up around the waterfront and has a potentially very attractive townscape which might draw many thousands of tourists if located in other countries, or even in other areas of Denmark. For most of its history, however, it has remained the site of the castle and a major marine centre, with cross Sound ferries, trading, and shipbuilding. Although the ferries continue, and a new terminal which further severs the town from the Sound has been constructed, shipbuilding has been in decline.

Though modified by the implications of the devaluation of the Swedish Kroner in 1993, the major source of incoming tourists is from across the Sound in Sweden. Although it is now difficult to imagine the extent of this trade at its height, it has current parallels with the beer runs across the English Channel between France and England. Prices, specifically for alcohol and for meat, were sufficiently low in Denmark to merit shopping journeys across the Sound, and many of the shops in the historic town centre were devoted to these two products. This had an evident impact on town form, leading, for example, to an expansion of butchers' shops well into the already crowded courtyards behind the traditional blocks. Whilst the trade still remains, it is now more modest. Figures show a decline in the number of hotel beds taken up, reflected in many other standard indices of tourist activity. The recent Swedish membership of the European Union may have further implications for trade.

There is still considerable attraction in visiting the town for the day (5 million visitors per annum claimed), for it is clearly Danish compared with the Swedish towns across the Sound. Nevertheless, it would appear that the local authority, which embraces a much wider area than the historic town and almost includes Denmark's major museum attraction, the art gallery and sculpture park at Louisiana to the south, has yet to make up its mind with regard to the form of future development. In this regard, it has many parallels with Oxford and with other towns in this study, where there is considerable local resistance to stimulating tourist activity. This is especially evident when the key planning investment of the past twenty five years is considered.

A clear priority has been on establishing new housing in the central area. The various mechanisms for building permission and development control steered towards the re-establishment of residential accommodation, even where retail or commercial accommodation had existed previously. Although, as

98

befits a major port for incoming visitors, the converted customs house, which is now a cultural centre, does contain a tourist information centre, this is possibly the only condescension towards visitors within the central area. The renewal of city blocks is essentially a private, local, affair done by, with and for the residents. There is practically no access for the visitor to the interior of the blocks in order to see the quite substantial changes that have been achieved, and the variety of green spaces that has been established. This is substantially different from many European cities, such as Prague for example, where the interiors of blocks have been opened up, with the establishment of public open spaces in order to spread the tourist load from neighbouring narrow streets.

Although visitors to Helsingor are expected to experience, enjoy and shop within the revitalised and resurfaced shopping streets, the amount of information available to them, on this quite significant urban renewal scheme, is limited. The visitor could possibly steer towards some of the key external spaces which have been redeveloped. There are pamphlets with illustrations, published trails and a poster, but in general (and rare for an historic town) the revitalised image of the historic town has been undertaken for the local residents. Insofar as tourism in Helsingor is concerned, it is Kronborg that counts.

Several other current planning proposals are likely to cause further public debate on the future of Helsingor and tourism within the local economy. Of particular importance is the future of the dockland area between Kronborg Castle and the Town. This is visually very significant, and consists of abandoned or underused wharf facilities, a small dockyard and commercial buildings in which some re-use has been achieved. The area is split in ownership between the municipality and the national government. With the reduction in employment to some two hundred, and what could be said to be a blot in full view of a national monument, there has inevitably been much debate concerning the area's future. The leasees, with some time to run, have brought forward a proposal for a mixed use area incorporating offices, a museum and leisure attractions directed towards expanding Helsingor's visitor market in a location clearly visible from the castle and the town.

The proposal has not found general favour locally, and has certainly not found favour with the national authorities responsible for Kronborg, who are reported as supporting a greening over of the area to provide an appropriate setting for Kronborg from the town. An international competition, largely focused on landscape design, produced a range of schemes which reintroduced the traditional lines of defence around the castle, provided parks and, in some submissions, residential areas. Within the town there is considerable interest, again in parallel with the policy for the central area, of establishing a new residential district with its supporting services and thereby bridging the gap between town and castle. The discussion over this area has gone on for some time, and within it there is a debate over sustaining past visitor volumes in a town of 12 percent unemployment, or turning the town's back against further visitors.

The process of revitalisation and careful guarding of local interests and of city life is, in many ways, a model for others to follow. Helsingor's problem is not how a surplus of visitors can be accommodated within the town, but rather how many visitors to Kronborg and Louisiana might be drawn to the town to its benefit. There are certainly visitors within the area, but much restructuring and promotion will be required to draw them to the town, and it is unclear as to whether the town really wants this type of attention.

Helsingor is, therefore, at a point of major repositioning for its product, re-emphasising the historic core and heritage attractions, and developing events to enhance this image. Its future, like that of so many heritage centres, is not entirely in local hands. The town provides an instructive example of the way in which local assets may be regarded differently by local and national interests. National (and international) designations for heritage are often based on cultural judgements which fail to take account of the crucial, and sensitive, role which such assets play in a more local economy. In Helsingor's case, several very different concepts of carrying capacity for the future are involved.

6.8   Bruges

Our host seminar city provided an immediate reference for the issues which emerged during the workshop. Recent survey evidence provided detailed data on the economic benefits derived from the more than half a million overnight tourists, and over two million excursionists, who visit the inner city area annually. This distinction, between those staying overnight and day excursionists, has been fundamental in the city's analysis of benefits, and in its plans for central area management and future development.

Like Heidelberg, Bruges (120,000 population, 1993) has taken steps to involve the community, and has highlighted major tourist related planning and management issues through its document, *A Livable and Lively Bruges at Stake: White Book of a Policy*, distributed to every household. The document shows the high level of integration already achieved between the urban management needs of resident and visitor communities. Jansen-Verbeke (1992) notes that such initiatives developed following overt opposition to tourism pressures in 1990.

Bruges has a more delicate central area morphology than, for example, Chester or Canterbury, and has suffered far less from postwar development. It is the heart of an affluent city region, standing fifth in the functional hierarchy of Belgian cities, but only eighth in terms of population. The entire central area, riddled with attractive streets and passages, is the essential asset. It is highlighted by sequences of dominant buildings and canals, and well provided with museums, shops and restaurants, whilst still performing the function of a central business district. A subsidy system for building renovation has existed since the nineteenth century, and a wide range of design guidelines and controls have evolved to ensure the quality of built form. The townscape is thus a considered response to the role of an historic city and visitor centre.

Currently visitor policies include:

. no further promotion of excursionism. Bruges no longer features in such programmes organised by the Flemish Tourist Board or Belgian Railways;
. establishment of a traffic free centre, building on the existing traffic management plan which prevents cars crossing the centre, reduces central speeds, and provides ring road linked underground parking. To this must be added the popularity of the bicycle (with ownership higher than Oxford) and an effective and expanding public transport system;
. new attractions established within the central zone;
. development of the conference market, and inner area hotels; and
. emphasis on events which animate areas, and encourage overnight stays.

Central Bruges is more clearly designed and maintained as a visitor destination than many cities, although care is taken to supply the needs of the local population. Despite policies to the contrary, however, the fringes of adjacent residential areas are increasingly influenced by core tourism. The city's representative talked overtly of the city's heritage 'product', and design and management are more evidently directed towards appropriate development of this industry. Street fairs, musical events, and special art exhibits are clearly promoted as visitor attractions, and more attention has been paid to the needs of the disabled, as with tactile models and texts adjacent to attractions.

The potential for extending visitor pedestrian routes is considerable, and canal tours serve to open latent walking opportunities to the visitor, rather as Chester's encircling wall provides a view of adjacent attractions. Of all the cities considered in this chapter, Bruges has developed the firmest spatial and programming policies based on a detailed knowledge of the visitor market. In doing so, it is creating a distinct product which will require a high level of investment, management and regular upgrading. Although day visitors are not to be encouraged further, it is not clear how current overcrowding in central sites is to be diffused. It is also unclear whether disincentives will, eventually, be required to reduce the unfavoured day visitor.

The Bruges approach emphasises:

. comprehensive visitor planning based on economically directed policies, and a clear highlighting of the city centre as a location for the tourism function;
. a direct view of the heritage city as a product to be marketed; and

. the importance of time management, through events programming, as an essential addition to the more common management of space. In this regard the presentation of the Hans Memling exhibition between mid-August and mid-November 1994 was indicative. It sought to both extend the visitor period, and the visitor range, through special trails and tours extending from the city.

The historic development of Bruges has involved a steady growth of visitors, with each generation reinforcing both the images and attractions of the place, and stimulating local management responses. Such responses are very much part of the political debate in the city and have, at times, been forced onto the agenda of democratic discussion through media attention, community action, and the reported inability of individuals to cope with more visitors in their everyday lives. These represent the safety valve for tourist carrying capacity, and ensure that tourism issues are incorporated within the fuller planning process.

Several commentators have noted the continuing pressures on Bruges and the need for further planning integration and political attention. Of these, Rondas (1992) provides a provocative conclusion:

'... the pressure on Bruges continues to be high ... a strict control may not be enough to protect Bruges' identity ... other measures must be taken ... stricter criteria to assess the impacts will be needed. A limit on the number/size of inner city hotels ... to halt the degradation of Bruges' identity. This needs political courage. On top of that, a more adapted planning system, capable of dealing with contemporary pressures, is needed. It may look unreal that in a rich, western country, structure plans cannot have any legal power at all.'

6.9   Conclusions

Whilst the sizes of the host communities, the numbers of visitors received, and the balance of day to overnight visitors vary considerably between the towns discussed, some interim conclusions can be adduced:

1. Whilst creative solutions to problems of visitor density require new methods of working, new structures and a willingness to innovate, they are only likely to be initiated by committed individuals who enjoy a marginal role between existing structures and organisations, but can create new opportunities.

2. More 'qualitative' attitudinal, environmental and interview survey data is essential to supplement the more 'quantitative' data which may be available on tourist activity. Such data provides an informed basis for the

102

establishment of the dimensions of local carrying capacity, and for the views of visitors and residents.

3. Carrying capacity issues embrace both the concerns of the physical and economic planning processes, and the strategic management of urban centres. There are implications for the extension of public planning processes and strategies to include aspects of visitor management and customer care.

4. Financial resources play a crucial role in the amelioration of problems posed by visitor numbers, and in the enhancement of visitor experiences. This is particularly significant with regard to nationally, and internationally, recognised sites where national policies for heritage management and support should exist aside from the more predictable investment in heritage conservation.

5. Whilst few towns can design their way out of major decisions with regard to visitor management, design interventions, when supported by viable survey data, should be seen as an opportunity to contribute to the infrastructure of the historic town. There is always room for the creative contribution which adds contemporary weight to the historic townscape.

6. New, locally developed, structures for visitor management and promotion are emerging from the relationship between the conservation and planning of historic towns, and the evolving process of high street management. The experience of such structures must be monitored and made internationally available.

7. The resolution of traffic problems through both regulation, and the provision of public facilities, is central to the local community perception of carrying capacity issues.

8. Effective public consultation towards the agreement and publication of goals for visitor management provides a basis for continuing debate and individual action.

What also emerges is that local circumstances will determine various paths to success with regard to visitor management in the historic town. For many towns, visitors are seen as an essential element in the new economic mix; others have resolutely turned their back on the implications of visitor development.

7 Tourism impacts and responses - the case of Venice

7.1 Introduction

Growing visitor numbers can have positive effects for a local community, especially in terms of income and employment, but, should the growth in local tourism demand persist, the pressure of tourism on the historic town may become excessive. The number of visitors reaches a level beyond the tourist carrying capacity, and negative effects may outweigh the positive advantages. Tourism is then causing damage to the local environment, the monuments, the local population, and even the quality of the visitor's experience.

This is the case in the historic centre of Venice. In 1952 more than half a million tourists spent 1.2 million bed-nights in Venice. These figures have grown to 1.21 million tourist arrivals in 1992 with 2.68 million bed-nights spent in hotel, and non-hotel, accommodation. In the same period, Venice has become a destination for a huge number of day-trippers: almost six million in 1992 alone. The island of Venice, a fixed area of about 700 hectares constituting the unique 'forma urbis' which still survives thanks to a series of special laws and the (loving) attention of the world culture, was visited in 1992 by more than seven million people (Figure 7.1).

Nowadays, tourists and residents are competing for the 'use' of the historic centre of Venice, which at present has less than 80,000 inhabitants, and receives up to 47,000 commuters daily. In 1951, Venice contained 175,000 inhabitants, a number which has been declining ever since. The exodus of population and economic activities has partly been fuelled by a process of 'crowding out' by tourism activities. It is therefore reasonable to assume that the number of visitors that Venice actually receives, is approaching, or has already passed, the tourist carrying capacity of the city. Venice may be seen

Figure 7.1   The historic centre of Venice

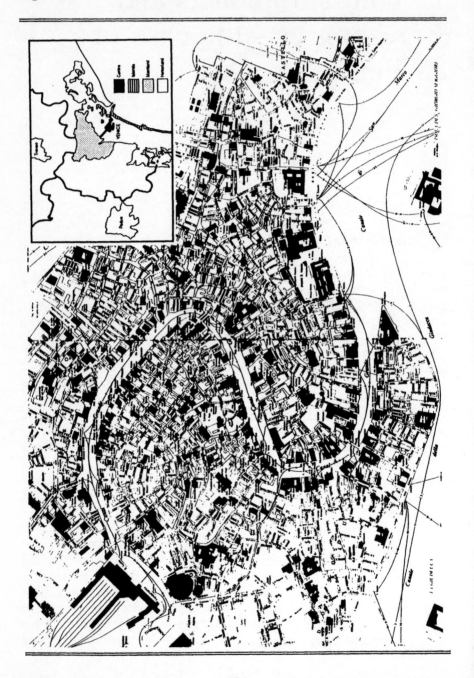

as an extreme case. But as the Europe-wide survey has pointed out, a number of other European historic cities are expected to share some of the problems that Venice has today, in the near future at least.

The scope of this study of Venice, is threefold. The first is to introduce the reader to some of the issues that underlie Venice's experiences with excess tourism demand. The second is to discuss three concepts of tourist carrying capacity that are the most relevant for Venice. These are the local community (social) carrying capacity, which reflects the perception of the inhabitants of Venice regarding tourism, the visitor carrying capacity, which starts from the quality of the visitor's experience and socio-economic carrying capacity, which seems appropriate for describing the conflict between the different socio-economic functions which the Venetian tourism system is performing. Thirdly, a brief description is given of how Venice seeks to manage tourism flows, both from a quantitative and a qualitative point of view.

7.2 Tourism in Venice

Together with its particular physical structure, tourism is seen by many Venetian commentators to be one of the principal causes of the persistent urban crisis in which the historic centre of Venice finds itself. Figure 7.2 describes the principal tendencies that characterise Venetian residential tourism (that is tourism implying at least one overnight stay in the centre), in the last few decades. It shows that the market for residential tourism, in terms of arrivals as well as overnight stays, has been expanding from 1963 onwards. While the total numbers of arrivals and stays for 1963 were respectively 759,975 and 1,731,440, by 1992 the historic centre of Venice had 1,208,946 arrivals and 2,680,179 stays. The growth was almost continuous until the second half of the 1980s, except for occasional standstills (for example in 1968). This growth in residential tourism which Venice experienced during the late 1970s and early 1980s still remained far below that of urban tourism and tourism in general in the Veneto Region for the same period (see for example Gambuzza, 1990).

In 1985 and 1986, a sudden decline in the number of arrivals and stays was observed. This 'crisis' can only partly be attributed to the massive withdrawal of the American tourists, an important segment of the Venetian market, from a vacation in Europe under influence of an unfavourable exchange rate of the US Dollar, and of terrorism. In 1991 a similar dip in demand was observed. In the 1960s, 1970s and 1980s, the number of arrivals grew somewhat faster than the number of stays, which led to a decrease in the average stay of the residential tourist. This shortening of the average duration of the holiday is a phenomenon observed on a global scale. More recently in Venice, there has been a slight rise in the average stay contrasting with the general tendency.

Figure 7.2   Residential tourism in the historic centre of Venice

Year	Absolute values		Change in %		Average Stay (Days)
	Arrivals	Stays	Arrivals	Stays	
1963	759,975	1,731,440	-	-	2.28
..	..	..	6.2	- 1.7	..
1968	807,175	1,701,816	-	-	2.11
..	..	..	13.4	9.2	..
1973	915,504	1,857,713	-	-	2.03
..	..	..	15.9	17.3	..
1978	1,061,416	2,179,730	-	-	2.05
..	..	..	25.9	30.6	..
1984	1,335,968	2,846,007	-	-	2.13
1985	1,291,878	2,768,655	- 3.3	- 2.7	2.14
1986	1,118,419	2,457,695	-13.4	-11.2	2.19
1987	1,129,734	2,486,572	1.0	1.2	2.20
1988	1,199,612	2,568,370	6.2	3.3	2.14
1989	1,235,001	2,662,670	3.0	3.7	2.15
1990	1,250,649	2,760,068	1.3	3.7	2.21
1991	1,111,456	2,508,595	-11.1	- 9.1	2.26
1992	1,208,946	2,680,179	8.8	6.8	2.21

Source: CoSES and APT, various publications.

Of course Venice is not only visited by staying tourists, but also by excursionists or day-trippers. Excursionism does not imply any overnight stay; the visit to Venice is concentrated within one day. Each year Venice is visited by more than 5 million excursionists. The relative importance of excursionism for the centre of Venice is indicated by Figure 7.3, which is based on estimations made by Manente and Rizzi (1993). They calculated the dimensions of the various visitor flows on the basis of the results of a survey of visitors in 1989-1990, and the enumeration of visitors at the principal terminals that give entrance to the lagoon city. (It should be noted that those visitors spending the night on the adjacent Lido have been considered as residential tourists in the centre, and not as excursionists.)

Figure 7.3 Tourists and excursionists: market shares in 1992

	Visitor 'Days'	% of Total
Residential tourists	2,680,179	31.1%
Excursionists, of which:	5,946,844	68.9%
Traditional	2,267,918	26.3%
Indirect	1,571,080	18.2%
Commuting	2,107,846	24.4%
Total	8,627,023	100%

Source: Manente and Rizzi, 1993.

There are reasons to believe that the number of residential tourists is somewhat higher than the official statistics indicate (principally due to tax evasion). Whatever the case, according to these estimates, the share of excursionists in the flow of visitors, on an annual basis, is not less than 65 percent of the total number of visitors (i.e. two excursionists for every residential tourist). There are three types of excursionists. Firstly, the 'traditional' excursionists who visit Venice from their home (26.3 % of all visitor days). 'Indirect' excursionists visit Venice from their holiday destination which is not Venice (18.2 %). 'Commuting' excursionists have Venice as a destination of their vacation, but sleep elsewhere, mostly for economic reasons. Hence, 24.4 % of the visitors to Venice 'commute'.

The share of excursionists in the total visitor number has tended to remain stable in recent years (see the estimates of CoSES (1989) made for previous years). It is, thus, not surprising that the local tourism industry is reorienting its supply towards excursionism. What we observe in Venice is a stagnation of the residential tourism market accompanied by an expansion of the market for excursionism. Costa (1990) has shown that, given an overall expansion of the market for cultural tourism and the limited and fixed supply of beds in the centre of Venice, the number of excursionists is going to rise considerably.

Figure 7.4 provides an explanation for the growth of an important part of the excursionist market, namely the so-called commuting excursionists can save money locating close to, but not in, Venice. The price of a double room diminishes with the increase in distance from the historic centre of Venice.

Padova, especially, seems to offer a competitive alternative to Venice, with a room in a 'four star' hotel costing 68 percent less. It is almost 40 kilometres away from Venice but this distance can be covered (centre to centre) in under 30 minutes. It is these enormous price differences that have given rise to the appearance of a 'false' excursionist, who considers Venice the final holiday destination, but locates in its surroundings to save money (or because inadequate accommodation in the centre).

Only by the disaggregation of visitor statistics can the dangers of mass tourism to a historic and vulnerable city such as Venice be appreciated (Costa, 1990). At the Lido, hoteliers charge the same price for a room as in Venice. This means that the Lido does not constitute an economic alternative for the centre of Venice. The seasonal pattern, and the structure, of demand for tourism on the Lido is not beach-like, but typically urban. This explains the consideration of the centre and Lido together in the previous analysis of the structure of the visitor flows.

Figure 7.4   **Relative average prices per accommodation category and locality**

Locality	5 *	4 *	3 *	2 *	1 *
Venezia Centre	100,0	100,0	100,0	100,0	100,0
Lido	99,1	100,0	101,8	98.4	123,8
Mestre	-	51,0	76,6	90,3	85,7
Marghera	-	46,0	70,3	87,1	78,6
Cavallino	-	-	60,4	80,6	81,0
Lido di Jesolo	-	37,5	61,3	77,4	85,7
Bibione	-	33,0	55,0	77,4	90,5
Mira	-	36,4	47,7	85,5	78,6
Padova	-	32,0	58,6	71,0	57,0
Abano	50,0	55,9	61,3	83,9	69,0

Source: Rispoli and Van der Borg, 1988

110

Figure 7.5   Tourism in Venice in the year 2000 - forecasts

Residential Tourists		Excursionists	Total Visitors	Total Visitor 'Days'
Arrivals	Nights			
1992 1,208,946	2,680,179	5,946,844	7,155,790	8,627,023
2000* 1,540,000	3,491,000	6,261,000	6,261,000	9,952,000
* Low Growth Hypothesis				

Source: Costa, 1990

Figure 7.5 provides a forecast of the number of residential tourists and excursionists that will visit Venice in the year 2000 --together with the figures for 1992. The forecasts have been made by means of an econometric model, which relates economic development to changes in tourism and excursionism demand, assuming, in particular, that an increase in disposable income has triggered the expansion of the tourism market. Two economic scenarios have been used as input for the model, an optimistic one and a pessimistic one. The latter is used and assumed to be the most plausible given the recession of the 1990s to date.

The table shows that, notwithstanding the fact that the forecasts are rather prudent, the pressure on the island of Venice is going to increase considerably, due largely to the growing number of excursionists, a market segment that is often neglected by the official tourism statistics. Since the expansion of the residential market is related to the use of hotel beds (occupancy rates are already high), even part of the forecast increase in residential tourism might realise itself in the form of excursionism.

Figure 7.6 shows that excursionists spend much less than residential tourists. A residential tourist spends on average Lir. 105,793, (about 50 Pounds), in the historic centre. Traditional excursionists spend Lir. 40,067 (19 Pounds), the indirect excursionists spend Lir. 81,858 (39 Pounds), while the commuting excursionist spends Lir. 104,062 (49 Pounds), of which a large part is on accommodation *not* in Venice.

111

Figure 7.6   Expenditure of the visitors to Venice

	Lir.
Residential	105,793
Traditional excursionist	40,067
Indirect excursionist	81,858
Commuting excursionist	104,062

Source: Manente and Rizzi, 1993.

It is the excursionist that gets most of the blame for Venice's problems with excess tourism demand. From an economic point of view the preference for residential tourism seems more than justified. Excursionists spend much less in Venice than residential tourists, and, as Van der Borg (1991) points out, their contribution to various social impacts is more marked than that of residential tourists. In summary, residential tourists are much better for the local economy than excursionists.

The case of Venice demonstrates that the strictly economic aspect should not be the first, and principal, point of concern. It is the management of tourism that makes excursionism a threat for the urban tourism system. This can be explained as follows. Residential tourism is, by definition, related to the supply of beds. This means that the maximum number of residential tourists that the centre of Venice may contain per day is explicitly limited to the total number of beds supplied (approx. 12,000). The price mechanism regulates residential tourism demand in the longer run. Furthermore, since many residential tourists book their hotel, information is available in advance on the pressure of residential tourism on the city. Peaks can thus be anticipated, and measures taken. Further, since local tourism statistics are based on hotel registration, monitoring of residential tourism demand is relatively simple.

Excursionists do not make use of a typical facility that might limit their number explicitly and regulation by means of pricing is difficult. The facilities that hinder arrival in Venice, such as specific means of public transport and parking places, can be avoided if necessary. Excursionists improvise their visit and this means that it is very awkward to anticipate their arrival. There is a lack of data on visitor characteristics and monitoring of excursionism is possible only through expensive surveys among visitors. Visitor management therefore needs to concentrate on the flow of excursionists. Here, the mechanisms that automatically regulate residential tourism are absent. Measures need to be designed for the management of the excursionist flows which substitute for those mechanisms. Determining the tourist carrying capacity of Venice is therefore of the utmost importance.

7.3   The tourist carrying capacity of Venice

The next decade is likely to see an increasing pressure of visitor flows on all heritage cities. It is not difficult to imagine that the individual city cannot support an unlimited number of visitors, and that the carrying capacity of historic centres must be more thoroughly assessed. The carrying capacity of a tourist destination can be considered at various levels, including the level of the individual attraction, and that of the destination as a whole. The specific character of the city determines which of the levels is the most relevant. Interviews with attraction managers in Venice indicate that, since the majority of the visitors to Venice do not use any of Venice's attractions but just wander around in the centre, the level of the individual attraction is not very relevant for analysis for Venice. It might be expected that a similar situation exists in well-conserved and well-restored cities such as Bruges and Rothenburg, which are attractions in themselves. Hence, this section concentrates on the tourist carrying capacity of Venice city centre as a whole. The analysis includes the perspective of the local community, and the perspective of the visitor. This is followed by an outline of a socio-economic quantitative analysis of the carrying capacity of the historic centre of Venice building on previous approaches used by the University of Venice, School of Tourism Economics (SET). The use of the concept of the tourist carrying capacity at the level of the individual attraction is considered more in the case study of Oxford.

The local resident community

Residents are an important part of the tourism system around a destination. They are one of the ingredients of what has often been called the 'hospitality' of a destination. The reaction of the inhabitants of a tourism city to tourism in general, and to tourists and excursionists in particular, determines the social impact of tourism on the local society and thus the social carrying capacity of the destination.

   Following the Oxford Visitor Study (Glasson *et al*, 1992), CISET organised a survey among residents in the Municipality of Venice. The survey was carried out by three final year students of the School for Tourism Economics, and lasted from 14 until 27 July 1993, one of Venice's busiest periods of the city's tourism season. The survey was conducted as follows: three areas were identified in the centre of Venice: (1) Rialto; (2) San Marco; (3) Academia (see Figure 7.1). The questionnaire was a straightforward translation in Italian of the one used for the residents of Oxford, and is to be found in Appendix 2. Just as in Oxford, the interviews were held on a face-to-face basis. Generally, ten interviews per area per day were held for 14 days. A total of 422 interviews were thus conducted.

The results of the survey were quite surprising. Venetians do not have the negative perception of tourism in their city which might have been expected. They acknowledge the important positive economic effects (income and jobs), and agree on the fact that tourism generates some congestion as well. Most respondents succeeded in recognizing the trends that have characterized local tourism over the past ten years. They perceived the 'massification' of tourism, and were somewhat worried by the growing numbers of excursionists visiting the city. However, the decreasing quality of life in the city is perceived to be more a function of the poor management of the Municipality, than of the excess tourism demand. This is also the reason for the bias in solutions proposed by the inhabitants of Venice with a focus less on suggestions for visitor flow management, and more on general guidelines for the management of the Venetian urban system.

The visitors

On considering the forecasts for the number of visitors to Venice, which indicate that total tourism demand for the centre will increase at least until the year 2000, one might conclude that the economic tourist carrying capacity of Venice has not yet been reached. This certainly is an erroneous interpretation of this concept of the carrying capacity. The composition of the visitor flow, rather than the absolute level, needs to be considered. In Van der Borg (1991) it has been shown that the composition of the flow tends to change over the well-known life-cycle of the tourist destination. The mix of 'residential tourists-excursionists' changes over the life-cycle. Mature tourist destinations are confronted with massive flows of more gregarious visitors, mainly excursionists. In such cases, the economic limit to tourism development for the 'up-market' visitors has been frustrated. The quality of their experience no longer compensates for the costs they would incur visiting the city. In contrast, with lower costs, the excursionists still arrive.

As we have already seen in section 7.2, Venice is a good example of a tourist destination where stagnation of residential tourist demand can be observed, while the total number of visitors still tends to increase. In Venice, the economic carrying capacity of the centre of the city has already largely been surpassed.

The University of Venice, SET, approach equates the socio-economic tourist carrying capacity with the total number of visitors that can be permitted in a city without hindering the other functions it performs; this dimension is closely linked to the phenomenon of 'crowding out'. Tourism in cities like Venice or Bruges tends to dominate the city functions; tourism activities push other activities or functions from the centre to the outskirts. The price for centrally located land explains the process of crowding out.

The problem of determining the socio-economic carrying capacity for the centre of Venice has been formalised in Canestrelli and Costa (1991). They introduced a 'fuzzy linear programming model', and calculated that Venice could bear about 25,000 visitors a day. Even if there is some room for discussion about the exactness of this figure, it must be clear that it is far less than the number of visitors that actually visit Venice on peak days (in some days of the year up to 200,000 visitors). The Canestrelli-Costa model expresses the conflict that residents and tourists have, using the same services that the city of Venice daily provides. The model maximises local income from tourism, and introduces linear restrictions regarding the availability of accommodation, catering facilities, parking facilities, intra-urban transportation, waste disposal services and the space available in Saint Mark's Cathedral. The way the model is structured is described in the annex to this chapter.

Figure 7.7 represents the number of days the socio-economic carrying capacity of the historic centre of Venice was violated in 1987 and will be violated in 2000. The number of days on which the social threshold is passed is forecast to climb to 216 days, a 45 percent increase. This means that for almost two-thirds of the year the local population is faced with an intolerable level of tourism pressure. Currently, of the three dimensions of tourist carrying capacity considered for Venice, the socio-economic one seems to be the most restrictive.

Figure 7.7   **Social-economic tourist carrying capacity violation**

Days per year	> 25,000	> 40,000	> 60,000
1987	156	22	6
2000	216	110	16

Source: Costa, 1990

115

7.4   Visitor flow management in Venice

Difficulties in identifying policies to control visitor demand are influenced, amongst other factors, by the fact that every city must be kept as accessible as possible for some specific categories of users, such as inhabitants, visitors to offices and firms located in the city, and commuters studying or working in the city. At the same time, the art city needs to be kept as inaccessible as possible to some other user categories (the excursionists/day-trippers in particular). A number of 'hard' and 'soft' options could be considered, some of which may be more applicable in the unique setting of Venice than elsewhere.

A possible hard measure of visitor flow control would be to close the centre of the art city to private cars, and to reserve the right to use parking lots, as well as that to stop at the relevant terminals, to the categories of non-tourist users of the centre. This, in combination with the rationing of the capacity of the means of public transport that bring the visitors to the centre, would allow the local authorities to manage the volume of the visitor flow. Such a policy might easily lead to disappointment and frustration among those visitors who are not able to visit the city as they would have expected.

A softer, and possibly more efficient, way of rationing of the excess demand, both from the city and the visitor's point of view, is the introduction of an advanced booking system. Two principal systems can be conceived:

(i)   The sale of service packages at the moment of the reservation, which might include meal vouchers, tickets for exhibitions and museums and discounts in souvenir shops. The acquisition of such a package could be mandatory (a type of entrance ticket), or optional, and thus only serve as an incentive for advanced booking. In the latter case the potential user must be convinced of the advantages which the package offers, and hence of advanced booking.

(ii)   The introduction of a 'City Currency Card', serving to all effects as a credit card, valid for the length of the visit, and with which goods and services in the city can be paid. The card can be issued in different forms to different types of visitors, in numbers that are fixed in advance. The personal credit card allows also for price discrimination according to the hour or the day that the card is used.

Both the city service package and the city currency cards could be organised in the context of a telematics network which permits long distance sales in real time, an immediate update of the availability, and the issuing of relevant receipts. Venice is currently studying the possibility of making tourists book visits to the city in advance. The introduction of the so-called 'Venice Card', which is a combination of the two reservation policies mentioned above, might offer the visitor an incentive strong enough to book a visit to the city well in advance. Visitors are invited to book their visit to Venice, and receive in exchange the 'Venice Card' which offers them a series of advantages and possibilities which are not accessible to visitors that do not book, although the latter still have access to the city. The number of cards issued will be equal to the most restrictive of the different carrying capacities of the centre of Venice, which seems to be the socio-economic one. Residential tourists will receive a card together with their hotel reservation.

In a recent article, Ermolli and Guidotti (1991) describe the conditions which have to be satisfied to guarantee a successful implementation of such a system. They come to the conclusion that from a technical point of view, the monitoring and the control of the tourist flows in real time does not create any problems. What is essential, however, is that all parties involved have to be convinced that the regulation of the visitor flows is indispensable for all the subsystems using Venice. A high degree of co-operation is needed among the different users of the system and it seems likely that this condition is about to be satisfied in Venice.

7.5 Conclusions

Tourism might easily become a major source of well-being for heritage cities, but only if tourism development strategies succeed in respecting the limits that are inherent to tourism. Sustainable urban tourism development is more than just a trendy slogan, as the results of our study have illustrated. The case of Venice clearly shows that tourism generates considerable benefits, but at the same time it also generates huge social costs. The implementation of both sustainable tourism development strategies, and the technologies that support these strategies, is a major challenge that has to be faced by the national and local governments of many European countries. It is beyond doubt that the management of flows of tourists will touch many European cities, and not only the city of Venice.

Problem formulation

The determination of the carrying capacity of Venice is pursued here by solving, as an illustrative application of the FLP approach, a stylized 'Venice problem' where:

- The Basilica of St. Mark has been assumed to represent the whole system of unreproducible resources that attract tourists to Venice. Since all residential tourists and day-trippers, with the exception of some repeat visitors, will almost certainly visit St. Mark's, its use level under condition of stress can be set to determine the 'ecological' tourist carrying capacity of the whole historical centre.

- Six tourist supporting facilities have been identified as relevant, because they cater to the basic needs of visitors (e.g. sleeping, eating, parking and moving within Venice), because each one could constrain the whole tourist capacity of the historical city, and because their expansion would impose actual and/or opportunity costs to the 'nontourist-dependent' population.

- Three types of visitors have been identified to compete for the 'tourist use' of Venice and to yield net benefits for the 'tourist-dependent' population. With the three types of visitors -tourists using hotel accommodation (TH), tourists using non-hotel accommodations (TNH), and day-trippers (DT)- the objective function of the fuzzy linear programming problem can be written as:

$$\max z = c_1 \, TH + c_2 \, THN + c_3 \, DT$$

where z represents total per diem outlays (which are assumed to be a good proxy for the net benefits paid by Venice visitors to the 'tourist-dependent population' in spite of income leakages to residents outside Venice), and c_1, c_2, and c_3 are coefficients representing average daily per capita tourist outlay for each type of visitor. The value of this objective function (for which aspiration level, b_0, is defined by the 'tourist-dependent population' together with its minimum acceptable level, $b_0 - p_0$) has to comply with some constraints of the form:

$$a_i \, x \le b_i + \Theta p_i$$
$$\text{with } x = (TH, TNH, DT) \text{ and } x \ge 0,$$

where bi is the 'aspiration level' -optimal, according to the 'nontourist population' - for the carrying capacity of the ith facility used by visitors to Venice; (bi + pi) is the value, to be considered insuperable - at which the capacity expansion of the ith facility becomes unbearable for the population of Venice; ai is the vector of coefficients measuring the level of daily use of facility i by each category of visitors; and $\Theta \in [0,1]$ is the degree of violation of constraint bi, toward bi + pi.

Model solution

This FLP problem can be solved for different value of Θ (i.e., for different grades of violation of the opposing aspiration level): for the objective function, which represents the interests of the 'tourist-dependent population', and for the set of constraints which represent the interests of the 'nontourist-dependent population' of Venice. If local public authorities can influence the degree of admissible violation, they will affect the objective function (the benefits) as well as the degree of violation of the various constraints or the costs.

The solution for $\Theta = 0$ is the one that represents the achievement of the aspiration level for all constraints and then of the 'nontourist-dependent population'. But the solution for $\Theta = 1$ defines a situation of 'ecological' maximum capacity, a situation that corresponds to the maximum tolerance level for the violation of each constraint and to the achievement of the aspiration level of the 'tourist-dependent population'. For all intermediate levels of Θ, both 'tourist-dependent' and 'nontourist-dependen' populations will only partially achieve their aspiration levels.

In the case of Venice, a fuzzy decision process would suggest the compromising choice corresponding to $\Theta = 0.39$. Both the tourist-dependent population and the nontourist-dependent population would enjoy the same degree of satisfaction. The 'optimal' solution could become a stable one if, taking into account the relative size of the two population subgroups, some form of compensation could pass from the tourist-dependent population to the nontourist-dependent one. This 'optimal solution' would admit to Venice 9,780 tourists who use hotel accommodations (with a rate of bed-occupancy of 89%), 1,460 tourist in other than hotel accommodations, and a daily maximum of 10,857 day-trippers.

8 Tourism impacts and responses - the case of Oxford

8.1 Introduction

The university city of Oxford is a major centre for national and international visitors. It is already one of the United Kingdom's most visited cities, ranked third in popularity on recent English Tourist Board (ETB) visitor ratings. Amongst the visitors are substantial numbers of international tourists, from mainland Europe, North America, Australia, Japan and many other countries. Rapid changes to the world political map, the advent of the Single European Market, and the opening of the Channel Tunnel in 1994, may bring even larger numbers of visitors to the city.

This chapter provides a case study which illustrates the pressures of tourism on this historic city, and outlines some management responses. Such diagnosis and prescription requires an adequate and up-to-date information base. Oxford City Council and the regional tourist board (Thames and Chiltern) conducted major studies of visitors to Oxford in 1974 and in 1984. This data was updated by the Oxford Visitor Study (Glasson et al, 1992). This recent study included a major survey of 4300 visitors to Oxford, 400 local residents, and 35 local businesses. The information has been further supplemented for this study by surveys of local decision makers and individual visitor attractions within Oxford.

The next part of this chapter provides an overview of tourism in Oxford. This is followed by an examination of approaches to carrying capacity for Oxford, from various perspectives. Different groups have different limits to acceptable change, and the perspectives of the visitors themselves, the local community, and the Oxford Tourism Forum, a group of key decision makers in the process, are examined. This also includes reference to the more traditional economic, socio-cultural, political and physical dimensions of impacts and capacity. Approaches to management, at the City of Oxford scale, are discussed. This macro-scale analysis is then complemented by more detailed studies of several specific visitor attractions within Oxford, thereby examining the relevance of the issue of scale.

8.2   Context: visitors to Oxford

Oxford

Oxford has a population (1991) of approximately 130,000, including 25,000 students at the University of Oxford and Oxford Brookes University. Higher education is a major source of employment in the city; other key employment sectors include health (hospitals), publishing, vehicles and tourism; as such, the economic base of the city is more diversified than that of Venice. The city covers an area of approximately 25 square miles (63 square km) mainly within the Oxford Ring Road (Figure 8.1). The University of Oxford, with its rich heritage of medieval buildings, is concentrated largely within an area of one square mile (2.5 square km) in the centre of the city. Within this area can be found most of the current key visitor attractions: University buildings (such as the Sheldonian Theatre, Radcliffe Camera and Bodleian Library), museums (such as the Pitt-Rivers and Ashmolean), many of the thirty or more colleges of the University (for example, Christ Church, Magdalen and Balliol), and attractive streets, alleys and other public spaces, with their shops (eg. Blackwell's Bookshop), pubs and cafés.

This historic built environment is set in the context of a very attractive natural environment. The Rivers Thames (Isis) and Cherwell run through the heart of the city, and through the major open spaces of the University Parks and Christ Church Meadows, and provide further visitor attractions. The historic built environment also shares the one square mile with the retail centre of the city. Here are the major stores (eg. Marks and Spencers, Debenhams, Selfridges), speciality shops, cinemas, theatres and some newer tourist attractions, such as the themed presentation of the Oxford Story.

Visitors: an overview

Numbers and seasonality As noted in Chapter 5, there is considerable debate around the issue of the number of visitors to historic cities, and estimates cannot be accurate. Estimates of the number of visitors to Oxford made in the Oxford Visitor Study (Glasson *et al*, 1992) were derived from calculations using information on visitor attendances at six key attractions (a University

122

Figure 8.1   Oxford city centre

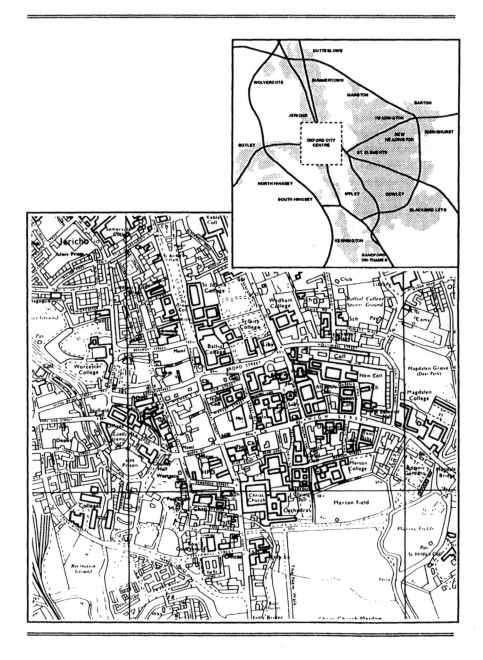

building/attraction, an Oxford college, three Oxford museums and the Oxford Information Centre), and results from the visitor survey on the proportion of visitors to Oxford visiting each of these attractions[1]. The average of the estimates suggested approximately 1.5 million visitors to the city in the study year (July 90 - June 91). This may be low as a guide in that there were particular conditions in 1990/1991 (Gulf War, recession) and a range of factors may increase the future flow of visitors to the city. An annual figure of 2.0 to 2.5 million visitors seems more likely to be the norm for the mid-1990's.

The gross number of visitors is of course a very crude guide to impact and pressure on capacity. The characteristics of visitor patterns can vary significantly with major implications for impacts. Of particular significance is the split between day and staying (overnight) visitors. Approximately 40 percent of visitors to Oxford are staying visitors, spending an average of three nights in the city. From attendance records of several visitor attractions it is clear that Oxford has a year round flow of visitors, but with two thirds in the period April to September and one third in the period October to March. Forty per cent of visitors to the city are concentrated in the July to September period. Allowing for the seasonal mix of day and staying visitors, there may be an average of 10,000-15,000 visitors in Oxford on any one day in the peak three months. This figure could be increased to possibly 30,000-50,000 on peak weekend dates. At the same period, July to September, many of the University students are away from the city, and this offers a partial counterbalance to the visitor influx.

Other visitor characteristics Some of the major characteristics of visitors to Oxford, derived from the visitor survey, are summarised in Figure 8.2. This shows the international attraction of Oxford, with a particular appeal to those under 35. Unlike many UK historic cities, only 50 percent of visitors come by car - but only one in five of such car borne visitors are currently persuaded to use the extensive Oxford Park and Ride service. The average spend per visit is boosted by staying visitors and much of this goes on shopping. The historic built environment in its various forms provides the attraction for visitors, but the most frequently named visitor attraction in the visitor survey was Blackwell's Bookshop. Apart from Blenheim Palace and the adjacent village

---

[1] Estimated numbers of visitors to Oxford = $\frac{\text{(Attendances at Attraction X)}}{\text{(\% of Oxford visitors attending Attraction X)}}$ x 100

For example - 2 million visitors during the year = $\frac{200,000}{10}$ x 100

Figure 8.2 Characteristics of visitors to Oxford (July 1990-June 91): Oxford Visitor Study

Where do visitors come from?
. 60%   UK
. 17%   Europe (including
         5% Germany
         4% France)
. 13%   North America (including
         11% USA)
. 10%   Others (including
         2% Japan)

What kind of people visit Oxford?
. 50% are under 35
. visitors do not bring children
. mainly in 'white collar' occupations

Why do visitors come to Oxford?
. 53% for leisure/holiday purposes
. 18% to visit friends and relatives (VFR)
. 10% for business/conference
. 8% for educational/language school
. 6% for shopping
. 5% others
(40% of visitors are on their first visit to Oxford; 30% have been at least five times)

Transport used by visitors to Oxford
. 50% by car
. 50% by public transport
(about 20% of car arrivals use the Park and Ride Service)

Day and staying visitors
. 41% stay in Oxford (threequarters within the City)
. 34% visit Oxford for the day from home
. 25% visit Oxford for the day from accommodation away from home, outside the Oxford area

Accommodation used by staying visitors
. 26% in hotels/B and B
. 36% visiting friends and relatives
. 14% with host families
. 11% in university accommodation
. 8% youth hostel/camping etc
. 5% others

How much do visitors spend?
(on average)
. £44 per person per visit (excl transport)
. £19 per person per day (excl transport)

What do visitors do when in Oxford?
. 54% visit an Oxford college
   (15% Christ Church
    6% Magdalen
    33% Others)
. 30% visit Blackwell's Bookshop
. 15% - 20% go to each of:
    Old Bodleian Library
    Ashmolean Museum
    Sheldonian Theatre
    Oxford Story
    Botanic Gardens
    river/meadows
. 10% take a walking tour of Oxford
. 10% take an open-topped bus tour
. 6% try punting

. 50% walk through each of four main shopping areas
. 25% use the Oxford Information Centre

Source: Glasson et al, 1992

of Woodstock, the other Oxfordshire towns, villages, natural and man-made attractions are scarcely experienced by visitors to the City of Oxford.

Visitors to Oxford can be disaggregated in various ways. There is an important distinction between staying and day visitors. Staying visitors are equally split between those of British nationality and overseas visitors; their main visit purpose is 'holiday/leisure'. They are largely first time visitors to Oxford and two out of every three arrive by public transport, although coach tours are not an important part of this figure. Staying visitors use a variety of accommodation while in Oxford and are an important group for expenditure in the city (approx. £21.40 per person per day). Day visitors fall into two categories. For those who visit Oxford from home, almost all are British as would be expected, over half have 'holiday/leisure' as the main purpose, but there are also some business/conference and shopping visitors. Almost 60 percent visit Oxford by car. This group spends some time in the city (50 percent spend more than three hours) and makes a significant contribution to the local economy (approx. £18.60 per person per day). Day visitors to Oxford who are staying in temporary accommodation outside the city are 75 percent overseas visitors. They come to Oxford for 'holiday/leisure' and arrive primarily by public transport (this group accounts for half of all coach arrivals). Over half spend less than three hours in the city (13 percent less than one hour) and they are the lowest spending group (approx. £12.50 per person per day). As outlined for Venice, it is this group which often receives much of the blame for bringing costs to the city, and with less redeeming benefits.

Another distinction is between British and overseas visitors. British visitors account for 60 percent of all visitors and 75 percent of those Visiting Friends/Relatives (VFR) and 75 percent of conference visitors. They account for most car arrivals and repeat visits, and spend on average £17.50 per person per day. Visitors from North America (primarily the USA) account for the largest number of those from overseas. They are largely on holiday and spend £28.50 per person per day. The other European visitors do not contain any one particular nationality. They are a young group (50 percent under 24 years of age), with an emphasis on visits associated with acquiring language skills as well as part of a holiday in the UK. They account for one third of all coach arrivals and spend on average £19.50 per person per day.

Visitor impacts: economic and social

Large numbers of visitors can bring additional costs to an area, including the crowding out of local economic activities (shops and public transport), and these are discussed more in the following section. There is also considerable economic benefit associated with the average visitor spend of £44 per *visit* (excluding transport) and £19 per *day* (excluding transport). The bulk of the

126

money spent (over two thirds) is on shopping and eating out. Only just over one fifth is spent on accommodation, with the remainder spent on other items (including entertainment and entrance fees). The pattern of spending reflects the importance of friends and relatives as a source of accommodation for staying visitors. The (minimum) total number of jobs supported directly by visitor spending in Oxford is estimated at 3000 to 3500, representing between three and three and a half percent of total employment in the City. Only about one in six of the jobs supported by visitor spending appears to be seasonal.

The amount of visitor spending varies considerably between staying and day visitors, British and overseas visitors and by type of accommodation and purpose of visit. A policy objective of maximising the number of visitor-related jobs created in Oxford, whilst minimising the number of visitors to the city, would focus on encouraging staying visitors especially in hotel and guest house/bed and breakfast/University accommodation; overseas visitors; and those coming to Oxford for educational purposes, to attend language schools, as part of a holiday and - perhaps - for business and conference purposes. Some of the social impacts associated with visitor pressures are noted more in the following section.

Visitor impacts: physical

Physical impacts are usually less well studied than economic and social impacts. The Oxford study has sought to include some information on this under-researched area. Supplemented by largely impressionistic literature and comment from elsewhere, they relate to an enquiry into the physical impacts of tourism in Oxford during the Spring and early Summer of 1993, and are grouped under the following headings.

Visitor density includes crowding, congestion, parking, pick up and dropping off points, meeting points and waiting areas for pedestrians and vehicles. The physical impact of pedestrian and vehicular crowding is evidently felt by regular city users, but is more difficult to identify or quantify. Oxford has developed an increasingly obvious programme of public space management, including daytime cleansing and high street management which leads to the early replacement of damaged street furniture and removal of defacements.

Habitat erosion including wear and tear on structures, surfaces and facilities; replacement and conservation of the physical fabric and vibration damage. Regularly used meeting areas such as Carfax (the historic road crossing at the city's centre) are inevitably worn faster than would be the case with only a local population, and there is some evidence that paving replacement is more frequent as a result of traffic and pedestrian crowding. There is also erosion to the stonework of frequented places, but this has not been raised as a major public issue. Picking up and waiting areas rapidly develop pedestrian crowding but no substantial erosion is evident from field checks.

Waste disposal includes toilet facilities, litter, rubbish removal and disposal. Public toilet facilities unfortunately provide space for a wide range of activities, some anti-social. There is no evidence that visitors to Oxford create other than normal pressure on inadequate facilities. It has been clear that outlets which particularly attract young visitors, notably fast food chains, have generated considerable street litter in the past, although joint authority/retailer policies seem to have reduced the problem. Litter is generated rapidly in gathering areas but is now cleared on a very regular basis. Discarded chewing gum in both public and private spaces is particularly disfiguring. There have been related complaints with regard to smoking discards in private and religious spaces.

Security includes theft, personal security and safety; traffic accidents; vandalism; pressure on police resources. Although the tourist literature has long identified problems arising from the presence of visitors in, or near, high crime areas (McPheters & Strong, 1974) popular perceptions as to increased crime from the presence of tourists as victims, or as language school students as offenders, seems largely unfounded. A survey of press reports revealed that few visitors were involved in security problems although theft is likely to be under-reported. In 1992-3 10 per cent of street crime was against foreign students, whilst under-age drinking, shoplifting and knife carrying were the most likely foreign student offences. Local perceptions of criminality may stem from the frequent presence in public space of tourists, foreign students and groups of homeless. The presence of a large student and visitor population, local charities for the homeless and the opportunities for begging attendant on tourism, create an immediate visual impact in some key locations.

General services include public transport; eating places; rest spaces and accessibility issues. Public transport and eating places obviously benefit from the custom of visitors. Use of Oxford buses is a matter of learned behaviour. Certain eating facilities are dominated by visitors, often international language students, at certain times. Public resting areas in Oxford are recognised as inadequate and visitors only aggravate a problem recognised locally. There are very few covered, or enclosed, spaces where visitors can shelter, but this is in line with a general national tendency to reduce the availability of unmonitored public spaces. Oxford, like most British cities, is gradually improving disabled access to public sites and facilities although access and signs still require attention. Foreign language signing is only slowly improving and no braille or other facilities for the blind (save for pedestrian crossing textures and sounds) are evident.

Environmental health issues include water quality and availability; air quality and noise levels. There is no evidence of pressures on these which can be specifically attributed to visitors. Nor did enquiries reveal specific visitor demand on health services. Indeed, an international population and excellent medical services provide a good response to any emergency. Similar visitor numbers might not be so well served in a heritage centre lacking such facilities.

Diversity includes visual evidence of service and activity diversity. Any visitor to central Oxford is made aware that the physical environment has been presented in response to the regularity and density of tourist visitors. Signs, retail offerings, the breadth of information evident, and the increasing customer care consciousness of public service staff are all positive signs of this awareness.

As a city centre with a range of attractions, rather than one focal attraction, the patterns of visitor use are distributed through a range of paths and spaces within the central area. The measurable physical damage reported from religious buildings and natural sites elsewhere has not become a matter of major public concern in Oxford. As a city with significant industrial, educational and service sectors, public utilities are more than equal to the to the task of catering for the normal demands of visitors.

It is clear, however, that smaller towns which rely heavily on the economic benefits of a visitor population can find their services under stress. This is especially likely when the acceptable local standards differ from those of visitors (as in water supply or waste disposal), where behaviour patterns of local and visitor populations differ considerably (as, for example, through religion), or where visitor numbers include substantial groups of the young, the elderly, or the disabled. Whilst physical impacts can be real, and damaging to the resource, they are often claimed by those seeking hard evidence to back up local prejudice occasioned by perceived visitor overload.

8.3   Carrying capacity: perspectives on impacts in the city of Oxford and limits to acceptable change

The resultant impacts from the interaction between visitors and the host environment can be analysed in various ways, including: economic/social/physical/political; adverse/beneficial; short term/long term; reversible/

irreversible. They can also be analysed from the perspectives of the key groups involved. This latter approach is used here.

The visitors

The visitor survey findings showed a positive overall perception of Oxford by visitors, although it should be noted that visitors to any town or attraction tend to note the attraction positively unless a particular problem has been encountered during the course of the visit. This general level of satisfaction is illustrated by the fact that over 80 percent of visitors said that they would like to make a return visit. Visitors to Oxford have had a wide experience of the UK's other historic towns. When asked how Oxford rated in comparison to these historic towns, fewer than 10 percent of visitors preferred Stratford, Windsor, Winchester, Canterbury, Lincoln or Warwick. Between 12 percent and 17 percent preferred Cambridge, Edinburgh, Bath and York. Overall, few visitors preferred other historic towns and over 80 percent of visitors to Oxford who had visited other historic towns, indicated that these towns were not rated higher than Oxford.

Figure 8.3 specifies visitor likes and dislikes about Oxford. People particularly enjoyed the architecture which, together with the traditions of the University and colleges, creates an attractive physical environment and atmosphere. The shopping facilities are also well liked and local people are regarded as friendly. The small-scale of the city centre was also regarded as a positive attribute. However that small-scale also underpins some of the dislikes. Although many visitors had no specific dislikes, other visitors made many comments, the most frequent of which were related to traffic and crowds. Almost as many people thought Oxford's facilities and amenities poor as thought they were good. Poor toilet facilities were a particular concern. Other comments related to the expensiveness of the city and poor signposting, as well as poor weather. Whilst the latter is beyond the city's control, its impacts can be ameliorated with covered spaces.

Oxford is still well regarded by most visitors and, using the definitions of Costa and Van der Borg (1991) already noted in Chapter 7, it can be argued that the city is still within its carrying capacity (the limit beyond which the visitor's experience falls dramatically). But as noted from the perspective of the visitor in Chapter 7, the mix of tourists can change. Capacity constraints for one mix will be different from that of another. Whilst Oxford has not experienced the dramatic shifts in the staying/day visitor mix experienced by Venice, reference to the earlier visitor studies does show a shift towards a younger mix of visitors.

Figure 8.3   Visitor likes and dislikes about Oxford

Attributes Liked	Number of Mentions	Percentage of all Comments (%)
Architecture/buildings	1982	31.3
Colleges/University/ history/tradition	1133	17.9
Physical environment/size/layout	1051	16.6
Shops/shopping	603	9.5
Atmosphere & people	569	9.0
Indoor attractions/activities/ facilities	329	5.2
Other comments	292	4.6
Nothing particularly liked	262	4.1
Don't know	113	1.8
Total No. of Comments	**6334**	**100.0**

Attributes Disliked	Number of Mentions	Percentage of all Comments (%)
Traffic related	1303	24.8
Crowding/tourists/people/beggars	703	13.4
Physical environment/dirtiness	236	4.5
Facilities/attractions	295	5.6
Expensiveness of Oxford	101	1.9
Information/signposting	51	1.0
Layout/size/too spread out	16	0.3
Other comments (poor weather etc)	220	4.2
Don't know	63	1.2
Nothing disliked	2257	43.0
Total No. of Comments	**5245**	**100.0**

Source: Glasson *et al*, 1992

The local resident community

The Oxford Visitor Study (1992) explored local residents' perceptions of the advantages and disadvantages of tourism in Oxford through open-ended questions and through the extent of agreement with statements about tourism in Oxford. Figures 8.4 and 8.5 show residents' responses to the open-ended questions. Of the advantages, more money (including foreign exchange) to Oxford was clearly listed most often, followed by increased jobs and trade, a more cosmopolitan and culturally diverse atmosphere, and the provision of more and better facilities. The main disadvantages listed were overcrowding and congestion, noise, litter and busy buses. Overall there is some evidence to suggest that, in the perception of local residents, tourism in Oxford may be near capacity. Fifty six per cent of local respondents felt that the number of tourists in Oxford was too high, 41 percent about right, and almost no-one felt that it was too low. However, local residents felt that the effect of tourism was positive (33%) or neutral (45%) rather than negative (22%).

There was a high level of agreement with the statements that 'tourism interferes with the residents' enjoyment of their own town', ' visitors result in unpleasantly overcrowded streets and other outdoor places', and 'tourists using Oxford's local transport system reduce the quality of service provided for local residents'. The verdict was neutral on the statements that 'tourists in Oxford erode the local environment and fabric of the city' and 'visitors' interest in Oxford's heritage means that our old buildings are better cared for than they otherwise would be'. Predictably, perceptions of advantages were more favourable by those who worked, or had a family member working, in tourism related jobs. Perceptions also had a geographical dimension; only respondents from the city centre felt that the problems visitors create outweighed their benefits in jobs and money.

The Oxford Tourism Forum

The Tourism Forum was established in March 1992, with the objectives of:

(i)   *providing opportunities for organisations involved in tourism located in the city to discuss tourism and other visitor matters to maximise the resources available for tourism;*
(ii)   *providing a catalyst for co-ordinating the activities of all those involved in tourism, to ensure that it achieves the maximum advantages to the local economy at minimum inconvenience to residents; and*
(iii)   *assisting with the development of a tourism strategy for the city and/or to comment upon such proposals.*

Figure 8.4   Local respondents' perceptions of the advantages and disadvantages of tourism in Oxford

Advantages	No	%	Disadvantages	No	%
More money	344	56	Overcrowding	372	38
Jobs	83	14	Congestion, longer queues	212	21
Cultural mix, Cosmopolitan	54	9	Noise	122	12
More/better facilities incl shops	48	8	Litter	104	11
			Busy buses	52	5
Increased trade	34	6	Crime	41	4
Better maintenance	25	4	Higher prices	26	3
Puts Oxford on the map	10	1.5	Fumes	18	2
			Bad pub service	11	1
More to do	10	1.5	Tour buses	10	1
			Other	22	2
TOTAL	**608**	**100**	**TOTAL**	**990**	**100**

Overall effect of tourism	No	%	The number of tourists in Oxford is:	No	%
Good	132	33	Too high	224	56
Neutral	178	45	About right	164	41
Bad	88	22	Too low	2	0
Don't know	2	0	Don't know	10	3
TOTAL	**400**	**100**	**TOTAL**	**400**	**100**

Source: Glasson et al (1992)

Figure 8.5   Residents' responses to statements about tourism in Oxford

		Agree	Neutral	Disagree	D/K	MOA
a	Tourism interferes with residents' enjoyment of their own town	360	16	21	3	0.9
b	Tourism brings more money to Oxford than any other type of business or industry	96	49	140	115	-0.1
c	Tourists in Oxford erode the local environment and fabric of the city	169	79	126	26	0.1
d	There are better recreation and leisure facilities for local residents because visitors help to support them	170	40	166	24	0
e	Tourists using Oxford's local transport system reduces the quality of service provided for local residents	308	42	33	17	0.7
f	Improving and managing tourist facilities in Oxford is money well spent	279	24	57	22	0.6
g	All the different nationalities amongst Oxford make the streets more interesting	174	64	161	1	0
h	Visitors' interest in Oxford's heritage means that our old buildings are better cared for than they otherwise would be	194	20	149	37	0.1
i	Visitors result in unpleasantly overcrowded streets and other outdoor places	365	20	13	2	0.9
j	Because of tourism, Oxford has a good local public transport service	29	18	342	11	-0.8
k	Jobs created by tourism are demeaning and of low status	96	28	245	31	-0.4
l	Visitors to Oxford interfere with local peoples' use of entertainment, leisure and recreation facilities	251	55	71	23	0.5
m	Visitors to Oxford bring jobs and money, and that is more important than the problems they create	184	40	155	21	0.1

* MOA = agree - disagree/(agree + disagree + neutral + d/k)

Source: Glasson *et al*, 1992

134

Members of the Forum include representatives of the City Council, the Chamber of Commerce, the local bus companies, British Rail, Thames Valley Police, the Oxford Guild of Guides, Hotel and Guest House Association, the Oxford Story, the Apollo Theatre, languages schools, Tourist Information Centre, Regional Tourist Board, Oxford Preservation Trust and the two Universities.

A questionnaire survey of members of the Forum, in 1993, sought to identify the views of this key group of decision makers involved in tourism and visitor activity. The 20 respondents had views very similar to local residents on the advantages and disadvantages of tourism in Oxford. The former were dominated by economic advantages (especially jobs, income and commercial opportunities); the cosmopolitan nature of the city was valued by many; the international prestige and the perceived greater variety of local shops and facilities resulting from tourism, were seen as other advantages. The main disadvantages were seen as overcrowding and congestion (especially from coaches, and during the summer months), litter and other forms of pollution, and disruption of the local community; the erosion of the physical environment, crime, and a 'cheapening of the image' of the city received an occasional mention.

The information in Figure 8.6 shows a much more positive view of the overall effects of tourism than that of local residents. The proportion of respondents perceiving the number of tourists in Oxford to be too high is much lower than that of local residents. The responses to statements about tourism in Oxford also reveal a much more positive perspective on the advantages of tourism. Members of the Forum were neutral on the question of tourism interference with residents' enjoyment of their own town, and on the impact on the local transport system; they welcomed the cosmopolitan mix of visitors in the streets and believed that the jobs and money brought by visitors were clearly more important than the problems they created.

8.4 Approaches to the management of tourism in the city of Oxford

A visitor management approach

Visitor management requires a clear view of the issues associated with visitors, a clear set of goals to guide action, strategic directions for action, and specific policy options to meet the goals. Visitor management cannot be detached from other issues, strategies and policies for the area/site under consideration. In Oxford, visitor management at a time of substantial employment decline (e.g. from closures in the motor industry) cannot ignore employment implications.

135

A recent (1993) study of Oxford's traffic problems also has considerable relevance for some visitor management issues and policies.

A number of *key issues* have emerged from the *Oxford Visitor Study* (Glasson *et al*, 1992). The issues are interconnected; some relate to the quantity and distribution of visitors in Oxford, others relate more to the type of visitor. Some are more important that others:

. *Traffic congestion: congested roads, visitor coaches etc.*

. *People congestion: crowds of people (in streets, attractions, buses etc).*

. *Concentration of visitors in centre of city.*

. *Conflict of activities and groups (eg. pedestrian-vehicle; inquisitive tourists-private academia; large groups-individuals).*

. *Nature of accommodation and attractions (quality, quantity).*

. *Environmental deterioration (litter, noise, fumes, erosion).*

. *Differential impacts of visitor types/groups.*

. *Leakage of potential local economic benefit.*

The *Oxford Visitor Study* proposed the following *goals* for a visitor management approach for the city:

. *Enhance the quality of the Oxford provision (eg. general natural and built environment; specific attractions and facilities) for both visitors and locals.*

. *Enhance the visitor experience.*

. *Improve visitor-host interactions.*

. *Increase local net economic benefit from visitors to Oxford.*

. *Reduce the physical environmental impacts and encourage environmental sustainability.*

To achieve these goals the Study proposed some important *strategic shifts* in Oxford's visitor management policies:

. *More <u>dispersal</u> of visitors, attractions and impacts, by season and location.*

. *More <u>targeting</u> of particular visitor groups (eg. staying visitors who bring more economic benefit).*

136

Figure 8.6   Oxford Tourism Forum responses to statements about tourism in Oxford

		Agree	Neutral	Disagree	D/K	MOA
a	Tourism interferes with residents' enjoyment of their own town	7	6	7	-	0
b	Tourism brings more money to Oxford than any other type of business or industry	4	3	10	3	-0.3
c	Tourists in Oxford erode the local environment and fabric of the city	8	2	10	-	-0.1
d	There are better recreation and leisure facilities for local residents because visitors help to support them	8	5	7	-	0.05
e	Tourists using Oxford's local transport system reduces the quality of service provided for local residents	8	3	8	1	0
f	Improving and managing tourist facilities in Oxford is money well spent	19	1	-	-	0.95
g	All the different nationalities amongst Oxford make the streets more interesting	17	2	1	-	0.8
h	Visitors' interest in Oxford's heritage means that our old buildings are better cared for than they otherwise would be	10	4	3	3	0.35
i	Visitors result in unpleasantly overcrowded streets and other outdoor places	9	6	4	1	0.25
j	Because of tourism, Oxford has a good local public transport service	8	5	6	1	0.1
k	Jobs created by tourism are demeaning and of low status	-	5	15	-	-0.75
l	Visitors to Oxford interfere with local peoples' use of entertainment, leisure and recreation facilities	2	2	16	-	-0.7
m	Visitors to Oxford bring jobs and money, and that is more important than the problems they create	16	4	-	-	0.8

* MOA = agree - disagree/(agree + disagree + neutral + d/k)

Source: Survey, 1993

- *More co-ordination of the policies of the relevant agencies (eg. local authorities, transport operators, attraction managers, and the University of Oxford).*

- *More spreading of the benefits between the various groups involved (eg. higher priority for local people).*

A variety of *methods* were suggested to achieve the strategic shifts to meet the goals identified. These can be broadly categorised as:

- Restrictive, including physical controls (eg. banning of tourist coaches from the large areas of the city centre; a rota system for college openings to visitors).

- Financial, including charges and incentives (eg. a levy on coaches, more charges for visits to colleges and museums, differential pricing for visitors and residents).

- Marketing, information and interpretation (eg. better signposting, planned trails, regional routes, off-season programmes).

- Planning, design, management and co-ordination (eg. better co-ordination of agencies involved).

Some policy options

A consideration of policy options must be in context. The Oxford visitor profile already displays many positive features with regard to the management of impacts. A high proportion of visitors travel by public transport and there is some spread across seasons. Visitors are generally well satisfied; over 80 percent intend to visit again. Many relevant policies are already in operation. For example, the Oxford Park and Ride system is one of the most developed of its type in the UK; guided walking and bus tours do seek to interpret the local environment for visitors and may provide some limited spread of numbers. But there are many more possibilities.

Figure 8.7 provides a structured summary 'shopping list' of possible policy options. These involve the application of the strategies and methods discussed to the identified issues. Figure 8.7 provides an assessment of the importance, feasibility and timescale associated with the various options. Those asterisked (*) indicate a number of possible short-term initiatives which may be feasible even in the 1990's climate of financial constraint.

Figure 8.7 Summary of policy options for Oxford visitor management - assessment for importance, feasibility and timescale to adoption

POLICY OPTION	IMPORTANCE			FEASIBILITY			TIMESCALE (years)		
	High	Med	Low	High	Med	Low	SR 0-2	MR 3-4	LR 5+
1 IMPROVE TRAFFIC MANAGEMENT									
a Spread by marketing	✓				✓		✓	✓	✓
b Encourage alternative modes		✓		✓				✓	
c Improve Park & Ride	✓			✓			✓		
d Control visitor coaches	✓				✓			✓	
e Improve signposting	✓			✓			✓		
f Some traffic bans	✓				✓				✓
2 IMPROVE PEOPLE MANAGEMENT									
a Spread by marketing	✓				✓		✓	✓	✓
b Better signing, trails	✓			✓			✓		
c Targeting of visitors		✓			✓			✓	
d 'Oxford Package'		✓			✓			✓	
e College policies	✓				✓		✓		
f Develop TIC provision		✓		✓			✓		
g Manage language school students		✓			✓			✓	
h Tourist tax		✓				✓			✓
3 IMPROVE PROVISION									
a More accommodation		✓			✓				✓
b More dispersed attractions		✓			✓				✓
c Facilities	✓			✓			✓		
d Market dispersed attractions etc		✓			✓		✓	✓	✓
4 INCREASE/SPREAD BENEFITS									
a Target high spenders	✓				✓		✓		
b Introduce charges	✓				✓		✓		
c Differential charging for locals	✓				✓		✓		
d Differential transport fares		✓			✓			✓	
e Promote tourism employment locally		✓			✓			✓	

Source: Glasson *et al*, 1992

Figure 8.7 (continued)   Summary of policy options for Oxford visitor management - assessment for importance, feasibility and timescale to adoption

POLICY OPTION	IMPORTANCE			FEASIBILITY			TIMESCALE (years)		
	High	Med	Low	High	Med	Low	SR 0-2	MR 3-4	LR 5+
5 ADOPT A CO-ORDINATED APPROACH									
• a Establish VMP	✓			✓			✓		
• b Local partnership	✓			✓			✓		
• c Policy co-ordination	✓				✓			✓	
6 PROVIDE RESOURCES FOR VISITOR MANAGEMENT									
• a Joint funding	✓			✓			✓		
• b 'Lever out' funds	✓				✓.		✓		
• c Take up ETB initiative	✓				✓		✓		
• d Visitor contributions		✓			✓			✓	
• e Reinvestment	✓				✓			✓	
7 MONITOR VISITORS, IMPACTS AND MANAGEMENT									
• a Regular monitoring	✓				✓				
• b Involve local agencies/people	✓				✓				
• DISSEMINATE STUDY FINDINGS	✓				✓		✓		

• One suggestion for an initial package of relatively important, feasible short term policies to improve Oxford's Visitor Management.

Source: Glasson *et al*, 1992

140

Implementation

Visitor management initiatives can be pursued under a variety of policy frameworks. As already noted, there has been a major traffic study for Oxford, which has suggested policies to ban traffic from much more of the city centre. The Oxford Local Plan Review (1991-2001) includes policies on transport and tourism, accommodation and facilities for staying visitors, and tourist information (Oxford City Council, 1992). For example:

Local Plan Policy TO3
The Council will encourage tourists to use the Park and Ride Service, in particular by:
(i)   providing travel, parking and tourist information at park and ride car parks and providing information about park and ride in tourist literature;
(ii) seeking clearer road signing to park and ride;
(iii) giving sympathetic consideration to provision of visitor accommodation in the vicinity of park and ride car parks where compatible with other planning policies.

Local Plan Policy TO11
The Council will seek improvements in the extent of information for visitors, including information specifically for people with disabilities about access, by the provision of better information, additional tourist information points, interpretative displays and pedestrian signing. Improved traffic signposting for tourists will also be sought were appropriate.

The establishment of the Oxford Tourism Forum also represents an important contribution towards policy implementation. The Forum has already been a catalyst for public/private sector co-ordination and joint funding. Recent initiatives include a more co-ordinated approach to central coach parking, visitor dispersal via new walking trails and an extension of bus routes, and the development of an 'Oxford Package' of linked activities, with joint ticketing.

Implementation does, however, depend on the attitudes of the key actors involved, and their willingness or otherwise to accept the implications of a management approach. The 1993 survey of the views of the members of the Oxford Tourism Forum provides some interesting insights (Figure 8.8). Whilst all the goals proposed in the *Oxford Visitor Study* are supported fairly evenly and at a high level, there is more variation in support for strategies to achieve the goals, with some concern from Oxford interests about relocation of tourism pressures outside the city centre and beyond. The variation in views is more marked on methods of management. There is a high degree of support for the 'softer' methods of better marketing, interpretation, planning, and co-ordina-

Figure 8.8   Views of the Oxford Tourism Forum on elements of a visitor management approach for the city

Members were asked to give their views of the following Goals, Strategy Shifts and Methods, ranking importance on the following scale:

4	Very important; essential
3	Important
2	Of little importance
1	Not important at all; irrelevant

Goals	Composite Score
. Enhance the quality of the Oxford provision (eg. general environment and specific facilities)	3.5
. Enhance the visitor experience	3.5
. Improve visitor-host interaction	3.5
. Increase local net economic benefit for Oxford	3.5
. Reduce physical environmental impacts	3.5

Strategy Shifts	
. Dispersal of visitors, attractions and impacts	
. By season	3.25
. By location	2.9
. More targeting (esp. staying visitors)	3.4
. More co-ordination of key agencies involved	3.6
. More spreading of benefits	3.2

Methods	
. More restrictive, including physical controls on access	2.8
. More financial (eg. charging for currently free attractions)	2.25
. Better marketing, information and interpretation	3.7
. Better design, planning and co-ordination in advance	3.6

Source: Survey, 1993

ordination. There is much less support for the use of 'harder' restrictive methods, and even less support for financial methods of management. Key actor rankings of the various policy options outlined in Figure 8.7 further illustrate the points. Whilst there is almost unanimous support for better signing, for more co-ordination and for regular monitoring, there is very little support for a local tourist tax, for charging admission to all Colleges, and for differential (higher) charges for visitors than locals for Oxford attractions and facilities. The exceptions to this general response are a general support for controlling visitor coaches via charges per visit, and the banning of traffic from larger areas of the centre of the city.

8.5 Carrying capacities: issues of scale - local site examples within Oxford

Case study sites

Figures 8.2 and 8.3 indicate that the University of Oxford's buildings and colleges are the primary attraction for visitors. The four case studies used include Christ Church College, the most visited college, the Ashmolean Museum, one of the most visited University buildings, and two other colleges, New College and Worcester College. These case studies provide a cross section of impacts from and responses to varying levels of visitor pressure. Interviews were undertaken with the person most involved in visitor management for each site, using a standard questionnaire.

Christ Church and the Ashmolean both have approximately 250,000 visitors per annum. New College has approximately 20,000. The figures for Worcester College are not clear, but probably less than those for New College. All the sites are encountering rising numbers of visitors. The numbers peak in the summer months, and have reached   per day at Christ Church; the 'resident' population of the college is 750 (500 students and 250 staff). Most visitors are on holiday and sightseeing and normally stay on site for less than one hour; a secondary reason for several visits is educational; this is particularly important for the Ashmolean.

Visitor impacts

The most significant negative impacts appear to be social, with the through-put of visitors clashing with the primary academic uses of the sites. There can be congestion and crowding of some parts of the sites, with associated noise and a damaging of the local 'ambience'. At Christ Church, which is also the location of Oxford Cathedral, visitors can disturb worship. There is a particular

143

clash at the time of the June examinations. There is an increased risk of theft, and the outcome of the social impacts can be some dislike of visitors by the normal users of the site.

There are also physical impacts. Litter is a particular concern and there may be minor acts of vandalism. The softer 'natural' environment appears more at risk than the 'built' environment, and respondents drew attention to the erosion of paths in the grounds of the colleges, and a tendency for some visitors to stray off the designated visitor routes.

Economic impacts are seen as positive at Christ Church where a charging policy now covers the costs of 12 staff involved in visitor management and generates a contribution to the maintenance overheads. Income is also a growing factor at New College, which has recently introduced a small entry charge. Worcester College and the Ashmolean do not charge. Several of the respondents also noted the PR value of visitors, for the University and for the site concerned.

Capacity issues and management responses

Whilst all the sites would wish to minimise negative, and maximise positive, impacts, only Christ Church faces significant capacity issues, associated with high numbers of visitors at particular times. It is also the site with the most well developed approach to visitor management, and the only one with a clearly documented strategy. Christ Church provides an interesting example of the use of a wide range of management methods. There is an initial differentiation between visitors who may enter free of charge from any entrance. These include those wishing to use the Cathedral, business visitors, past and present members of the College, and local people with passes. Other visitors are directed to a turnstile entrance adjacent to Christ Church Meadow where they are admitted on payment of the appropriate charge, which is normally £2 for adults. The turnstile entrance point also provides guidance to those bringing groups of visitors (see Figure 8.9), and information leaflets for all visitors. The leaflets include useful information on the College site, details of the designated visitor route and a brief set of rules. The latter are reinforced by a team of custodial staff. No organised group or party larger than 25 people is admitted at any time; groups of non-adults must be supervised by at least two adults. Portable communication is used to monitor congestion at certain points, and admissions can be suspended to allow congestion at pressure points to subside.

A site such as Christ Church can use methods which are more difficult to apply at the level of the city as a whole, with more emphasis on financial and restrictive approaches. The site can be closed if necessary. Visitor routes are closely controlled, and guides are only permitted to instruct their parties at certain locations where the noise impact is more limited. Larger groups can be asked to split into smaller groups, which is difficult to implement in a city as a whole.

The case studies also illustrate the interdependency of sites and cumulative capacity issues. Several colleges are introducing charges, including New College which has a £1 entry fee (1993). This can divert visitors to those, such as Worcester College, which do not charge. Some attractions may deliberately become interdependent. New College operates a joint ticketing facility with Magdalen College and the Oxford Story attraction.

8.6   Conclusions: carrying capacity as a flexible concept

The impacts of tourism on a centre of cultural heritage such as Oxford have many facets. Some impacts, primarily economic, are seen as benefits; others, primarily social and physical, are seen as costs. Perspectives on impacts and on the capacity of the city to absorb such impacts vary with the perspective involved. The views of visitors and the local community, neither of which are homogenous groups, have been discussed in this chapter. The Oxford Tourism Forum (including business and community interests) could be used to gauge a co-ordinated view on the limits to acceptable change in the city. The current view of this group tends more towards targeting of visitor types (esp. staying visitors) and seasonal spread, encouraged by the softer methods of marketing and co-ordination and planning. Attitudes to restrictive and financial methods are less enthusiastic. Similar views can be found in some of the sites within the city, but at the most pressured sites there has been a willingness to use more controls - which are admittedly easier to use for a walled college than for an open access city. Capacity is a flexible concept, which varies between dimensions (eg. economic, social), groups and scale.

9 Conclusions

9.1 Introduction

This final chapter seeks to draw together some conclusions from the conceptual studies, and from the various levels of case studies. A key initial conclusion is the need for diagnosis before prescription! The early sections of the chapter focus on the lack of understanding of the pressures and impacts associated with visitors to historic towns and cities. The flexibility of the concept of carrying capacity, with its various dimensions and perspectives, is also re-emphasised.

The discussion then turns to some of the key strategic choices and methods involved in visitor impact management. The extent to which visitor impact management should seek to (i) concentrate, and (ii) target, visitors and their impacts provides the focus of the discussion of strategic choices. Methods to achieve visitor management objectives can vary from the 'hard' (eg. restrictive/financial) to the 'soft' (eg. marketing/co-ordination-planning) and the studies discussed in this book provide some interesting insights to the relevance and applicability of such methods. The final sections of the chapter draw out, briefly, some of the policy options which appear to be examples of current good practice. The importance of an integrated approach to visitor impact management, and of strategies, methods and policies which can be implemented, are stressed. The chapter concludes with a call to build on the important networks established in this research, for the further development of across-Europe understanding of visitor impact issues and management responses in historic towns and cities.

9.2   Understanding the problem

One of the more significant conclusions evident in this research is the lack of detailed information on tourism activity available to local tourism agencies. An extreme manifestation of this is the very limited availability of empirical data on visitor numbers, visitor activities and visitor patterns. Although the survey data shows that 'tourism' research has been undertaken in various towns and cities, it would appear that the focus has been primarily on economic issues, with some additional, limited, assessment of traffic problems. Tourism management is much more than marketing and information services, job creation or traffic management. Because of the emphasis placed on these aspects, very little comprehensive data exists, particularly at the local level, which highlights both the costs and benefits of the industry and the implications of using resources in various ways. As a consequence, tourism often takes a relatively low priority in most local government management activity. If the problems of tourism capacity are to be more fully addressed, a prerequisite is a significant improvement in the analysis of tourism issues, leading to an improvement in the level of knowledge which informs understanding of the problems of exceeding capacity dimensions. There is also a need to review the priority given to tourism in the management of towns and cities.

The data analysis should cover the various dimensions and perspectives noted in Chapter 4. Ideally this involves survey work covering visitors, local residents, the business sector and local decision makers. Such surveys should be designed to acquire not only quantitative information (eg. on numbers and characteristics of visitors, their travel and expenditure patterns), but also qualitative, perceptual, information on the benefits and costs of the visitor/tourism activity in the town or city concerned. Such data also needs to be updated regularly. Too many visitor studies occur at long and irregular intervals. Regular monitoring of visitor flows and their impacts is essential. Such monitoring will provide comparative data over time. There are also advantages in comparative analysis across similar types of towns and cities. Whilst every heritage location has its unique features, there are also many similarities in the nature of problems and in the management options.

Tourism is a multi-dimensional industry, with no clear authority or regulation over supply and demand. It is highly fragmented, and the distribution of costs and benefits are uneven, and often unclear. Although tourism does create jobs and income, the magnitude of these positive effects is dependent on how well the local tourism industry and infrastructure are integrated (eg. how much of the benefit leaks out to external suppliers?) If tourism is to enhance its positive attributes while limiting the consequences, it needs to have a higher profile in the day-to-day management activities of local government. When issues relevant to tourism in other spheres of local government are discussed, the impact on the industry must be considered. Currently, tourism is often considered in relative isolation, and primarily in terms of its economic and physical impacts. The resulting 're-action' to excess capacity, not necessarily only due to tourism, may result in imposed solutions which shift the problems to other areas or to another frame of reference, whilst still failing to address the root problems. If the use of tourism capacity is to have any value for visitor impact management, it needs to be underpinned by an analysis of the industry which goes well beyond the level currently practised and which includes all the components discussed in Chapter 4.

9.3 Carrying capacity, limits of acceptable change, and visitor impact management

This research has argued that the predominant emphasis placed on economic and physical thresholds of tourism is flawed. Capacity limits vary from place to place and from time to time, and depend on whose point of view is used in the assessment. In ecological and physical terms it is more often that a perceived breach of capacity takes place long before any tangible limit is reached. Capacity limits (defined by dimension, or by perception) may be screened in by a whole variety of factors including size of location (eg. physical capacities may be clearly reached in small/contained (eg. walled) sites, but less clearly so at the city scale); sensitivity of the natural or built environment (eg. natural environments may be more fragile than built environments - and in this respect some historic towns and cities may be more robust than rural locations); and the balance of visitor and local characteristics (eg. visitor/local population ratio, visitor/local age mix, visitor/local nationality mix). Capacity is a flexible concept and its purpose is not to say exactly when any site or city is full, but rather when the marginal costs of tourism are likely to exceed the marginal benefits and when serious problems begin to appear. This is why many now prefer to discuss a destination's capacity to absorb tourism and the limits of acceptable change (LAC) and how this can be applied to visitor impact management (VIM).

The LAC approach strives to define those conditions which are deemed desirable in an area and sets up management strategies to achieve specified goals. This approach does not look for use limits or numeric ceiling values, but uses the concept of land-use zones where a set of desired conditions in terms of social, ecological, physical and economic impacts are maintained. Standards are set, and indicators employed, to identify when unacceptable impacts emerge, with subsequent actions taken to modify the situation in line with management objectives. Indicators may relate to the various components of tourism impacts discussed earlier in the report including, for example, traffic and people congestion, tourism employment, and resident and visitor satisfaction.

Visitor impact management follows on from LAC; the VIM approach establishes what are considered to be unacceptable visitor impacts, determines the likely cause of these impacts, and sets in motion a series of actions to address the problems. Significant to this approach is a response to the dynamics of the industry which involves a long-term outlook. Like LAC it does not seek to achieve some numeric value that is approached with impunity, but rather identifies a set of standards which can be used to compare with existing conditions. Visitor impact management is a process of adaptation which describes desirable conditions and evaluates current activity as a basis for setting tourism management objectives. It does not consider tourism in isolation, but integrates the industry within other socio-economic development activity, thus forming an element of comprehensive local (and regional, as appropriate) development plans.

9.4   Visitor impact management: strategic choices

A clear finding from the Europe-wide survey of historic towns and cities is the constant underestimation of the issue of sustainability of tourism by both the public and the private sector when determining the tourism development strategy. In most cities there is something that resembles such a strategy. Often this does not go much further than the packaging of a number of promotion plans for the city and for some of its principle attractions. This notion, that tourism policy simply equals promotion has to be considered inadequate for today's tourism. In vulnerable urban environments, such as the European heritage centres, the tourism development strategy must deal with visitor impact management. This normally involves several strategic choices.

The first choice regards the decision between *concentrating or spreading tourism*. The tourism 'product', 'vacation' or 'excursion', is a composition of several products, in the sense that it is built up by many different, interdependent, tourism products. These sub-products are either attractions (primary tourism products) or facilities (secondary tourism products). While the attractions move the visitor, the facilities render them accessible. Many attractions are offered at very specific locations. Outside their local environment they would not have the same value to the visitors. Not only are many attractions concentrated in space, some of them are also concentrated in time. In space, tourists will visit the 'musts' more frequently than the lesser known attractions. In time, tourist demand still reflects traditional seasonal vacation patterns that follow the weather (sun, snow) and school holiday periods (summer break, weekends). Concentrations in both space and time thus seem inherent to tourism.

Some of the tourism destinations that have been included in the survey - Bruges is a good example - deliberately leave their tourism concentrated in specific zones ('golden triangles') and periods (peak seasons); with policies limiting the spread of tourism. Such a strategy allows areas that are not yet 'contaminated', and the periods of the year that are still quiet, to be maintained as such. The inhabitants then have the choice to knowingly locate in the area that is often congested by tourism, or locate elsewhere and not be bothered by visitors. During the quieter periods of the year the local residents have more of the city for themselves.

Those who argue for the spreading of tourism in space and time, assume that doing so will relieve the areas that in certain periods of the year are flooded with visitors. Visitor numbers thus remain within the limits in all areas, and social costs related to excess demand disappear. Furthermore, more inhabitants and local firms have the opportunity to profit from tourism. Some theoretical evidence that supports the effectiveness of spreading demand in time has been gathered for Venice, where the levelling out of seasonal fluctuations in visitor numbers is estimated to make the tourist carrying capacity per day compatible with the overall demand on a year basis.

On the other hand, Venice also demonstrates that the spreading of demand in space does not necessarily lead to a permanent relief of the congested parts of the local tourism system. It is not easy to persuade visitors to follow alternative routes. They need to be informed well in advance, and the alternative attractions must seem worth a visit. In any case, those that decide to follow such alternative routes sooner or later return to the 'musts'. The Oxford case suggests that while the introduction of an entrance fee for several colleges may lead to more control of the congestion problem of the single attraction, it may also transfer it to other attractions that do not (yet) charge. The phenomenon of transferring the problems from one part of the tourism system to the other is felt by more cities than Oxford. The Oxford case also raises the issue of willingness to support spread. Whilst there may be some support by the local business community and by local decision makers to spread the season (ie. in time) there may be less willingness to spread in space outside the immediate environs for fear of losing local economic benefits.

A second strategic issue relates to the *targeting of visitors*. Tourism demand is far from homogeneous. Within the overall demand there are segments that are socially and economically more or less attractive to the heritage centre. The tourism development strategy of a heritage site or city might exclusively, or predominantly, focus on those segments that are considered most attractive, for the objective of maximising benefits and/or minimising costs. The results of the case studies suggest a clear focus on residential tourists. They not only spend more on a per day basis than day tourists, but usually generate less costs as well. Furthermore, residential tourists frequently book rooms before leaving home, which makes them more manageable than day tourists, who improvise their visit. A further targeting of demand is possible by concentrating on very specific segments of the market, for example on conference, or on Japanese, tourists. The spending levels of these two examples are far above average. Whilst from a community point of view, the focusing on residential tourism demand may be effective for many elements of the local tourism industry, a further and more specific diversification of the marketing policy may merely favour specific parts of the tourism system.

It must be stressed that selective marketing is more than organising specific promotion campaigns. Selective marketing means developing specific products and attractions and adopting a specific price policy. This means, for example, that where a city has decided to shift the residential/day tourism mix towards residential, enough entertainment in the evenings must be provided and the range of hotel rooms should cater for a broad range of tourists. Where a city is seeking to boost its conference visitors, it may need to improve its conference centre facilities.

A visitor management strategy may target visitor demand, local attractions and facilities supply, or both demand and supply sides of the local tourism market. Where supply has proved to be relatively rigid, the reduction in the number of visitors or their dispersion must be considered. Where demand seems to be relatively insensitive to restrictive measures or price incentives, interventions in supply, for example by removing known bottlenecks, may have priority. The key strategic choices depend on the specific circumstances in which cities, sites or attractions find themselves. What this means for the way in which visitor impact management can be given shape is now discussed.

9.5 Visitor impact management: methods

Two lines can be followed to implement chosen strategies and to guide visitor flows. The first is what can be called the 'hard' line; the second is the 'soft' line.

The methods that belong to the *'hard' line are physical and/or financial restrictions* on the access to sites and cities. Several examples of physical restriction can be identified. The closure of a site or an attraction that is suffering from excess pressure of visitors is one of the most extreme measures that can be taken. The closure of an entire heritage city is much more problematic. Not only are there many practical problems that have to be considered, but also various legal problems. Venice has experienced on several occasions - eg. Venice Carnival, Pink Floyd Concert - the complete closure of

152

the inner city. A whole range of less extreme reductions in the accessibility to cities, sites and attractions exists. Examples include Park and Ride schemes, pedestrianisation of central areas, restrictions on coach access, selective parking, and the creation of artificial queues in previously selected nodes in the routes. Financial restrictions to accessibility usually integrate with the physical ones. Entrance fees, price discrimination between residents and visitors, and between different types of visitors for sites and attractions, prices for parking and public transport (shuttles between parking and heritage centres in particular) are but a few examples.

Since accessibility is a crucial precondition for tourism (and especially for excursionism), the 'hard' line seems, initially to be, the most effective. On the scale of the individual site or attraction it can help to manage visitor flows, but on the scale of the city the effectiveness of hard measures can prove to be marginal. Firstly because the visitors, when confronted with restrictions of any kind, almost automatically and immediately find ways to avoid them, with the obvious result that the problems shift to another part of the system. A positive result is not always achieved. In Venice a halt on the expansion of the supply of hotel beds decided some 15 years ago did not stop overall demand from growing, but caused a decrease in the quality of demand. In Salzburg the introduction of a traffic plan which limited considerably the access of coaches to the inner city made German bus operators decide to exclude the city from the list of destinations offered. This had immediate effects on the performance of the local tourism industry. The authorities where obliged to change the traffic plan. In some cases hard measures may be too effective, completely undermining the city's or site's development potential. Secondly, heritage cities can be seen as belonging to humanity, as when they seek designation as UNESCO World Heritage Sites, and access should not be overly restrictive. Indeed some 'hard' measures in some situations may be seen as unconstitutional, inequitable, and possibly illegal.

'Soft' measures include marketing, planning and co-ordination. As revealed in the cases of Oxford and Venice, but also elsewhere, such measures are normally preferred by the key actors in local tourism. It is usually easier to achieve a consensus for such measures. Once visitors, operators and residents perceive some common interests, their behaviour is likely to be more sensitive to the different dimensions of carrying capacity. Soft measures seek to guide behaviour to achieve the tourism objectives for the city or the site. At a very local level, better signing may spread visitors away from congested areas. Good marketing of for example 'Winter-breaks' may spread the season. A facility such as the Venice Card may persuade the improvising excursionist to book the day trip to the city, and hopefully to change plans if there are no cards available for the intended visit day.

'Soft' and 'hard' measures are not mutually exclusive. 'Hard' measures are normally more relevant and easier to apply at the level of the individual site. In that a city may include such sites, it may use both hard and soft measures. Cities may also use some city-wide restrictive and financial measures, particularly in relation to traffic management. But problems may not be solved permanently by hard measures alone. They may be shifted elsewhere, often temporarily or they may give rise to new problems, including the undermining of the economic potential of tourism, which is unlikely to satisfy the tourism objectives of the city or site. In general, soft measures may be needed to complement hard measures and may be more relevant, feasible and acceptable for the city as an entity.

9.6 Visitor impact management: policy options

Examples of detailed policy options have been raised in the case studies, and in particular for Oxford and Venice. This section draws together some of the contemporary initiatives under the three broad headings of traffic management, people management, and co-ordination, integration and implementation.

The better *management of vehicular traffic flows* is a high priority issue for historic towns and cities in Europe. The Europe-wide survey identified the centrality of problems of traffic congestion, and coach and car parking. Widespread management responses include the use of shuttle buses from primary distributors (such as railway stations and coach parks) into heritage centres, the use of coach drop-off and pick-up points, and pedestrianisation of heritage cores. Several of the case studies illustrate the advantages of keeping coach/touring car transport well outside the heritage core. Cities and towns with walls have an advantage in this respect.

Park and Ride schemes are also in good currency. The Oxford scheme is well established and considered one of the better schemes, but even here it is ignored by a large proportion of visitors. Traffic management measures need to be well publicised, and user friendly. The suggested measures for developing the Heidelberg park and ride are of particular interest (ie. park and ride areas will be signposted extensively, will be designed as reception areas with information terminals and facilities for hiring bicycles, and will have excellent connection to public transport that can be used by the disabled; some park and ride areas will be reserved for cars with number plates from outside the region; use of the 'environment co-operative' transport will be encouraged for links to the centre).

The better *management of people flows* is also a high priority issue. The Europe-wide studies and case studies illustrate problems of crowded public spaces, crowded local facilities and varying types of visitor-host interaction, with emerging problems of visitor dislike by residents of particularly congested locations. The minimum response by most heritage centres in the provision of free maps. This basic level of guidance has been supplemented by a wide range of innovative schemes in some locations. At the heart of such schemes is the provision of good interpretive detail, designed to enhance the quality of the visitor experience. An uninformed visitor will display uninformed behaviour. There is a need to avoid the rapid 'consumability' of heritage locations. Visitors should be encouraged to explore locations, although the Heidelberg tourism guidelines add a cautionary note and signal the importance of maintaining a 'residents' bonus' (safeguarding intimate local areas and features).

Good signing and high visibility marketing programmes, including leaflets, are essential. Canterbury provides good examples of trails and walkways which serve both residents and visitors. Bruges illustrates the use of street events to guide and manage visitor flows. The proposed 'Venice Card' provides a more sophisticated approach to advance management of people flows. 'Harder' financial and control measures may be used for specific sites/attractions within historic towns and cities. Paradoxically, the Europe-wide survey revealed that over a quarter of the towns and cities surveyed also used a tourist (primarily a bed) tax, which could be seen as discriminating against the very staying group which towns and cities are so keen to target!

The importance of a *co-ordinated and integrated approach* to visitor management cannot be over-stressed. Whilst many historic towns and cities claim to have a strategy, not many have visitor management at the top of their list of objectives. Visitor impact management requires the bringing together of an array of participants. There is great value in working in partnership, with configurations of interested parties including the public and private sectors, non-government organisations, and, hopefully, local residents. The case studies provide some interesting examples. In Oxford, the Oxford Tourism Forum has created a new public-private sector partnership; in Canterbury and Chester, the City Councils have taken an important lead. The Canterbury experience also highlights the close relationship between land-use planning, traffic management and visitor management processes. Heidelberg exemplifies the importance of involving local people if the local community is to recognise the economic and cultural value of tourism. Whilst Bruges, and other locations, emphasise that a heritage city is a 'product' to be marketed, good practice should now recognise that the traditional tourist promotion agency is not a sufficient vehicle to handle the essential and wider visitor management issues facing historic towns and cities.

A co-ordinated and integrated approach will facilitate the implementation of a visitor management strategy. It is essential that such an approach is underpinned with up to date information. The regular monitoring of visitor characteristics and their impacts is vital, but is currently a very weak link in the process. With better information, visitor management can be more proactive and capacity issues can be better anticipated and responded to. The alternative reactive approach may lead to panic responses, crisis 'management', and an alienation of visitors and residents alike.

9.7 The importance of networking and of comparative studies

This book has made considerable use of comparative studies at several scales, ranging from the Europe-wide questionnaire survey, through the set of cathedral, university and trade city case studies, to the detailed Oxford and Venice studies. There is much to be gained from networking and comparative studies. The English Historic Towns Forum (EHTF) provides a good example at the national level. Founded in 1987, the EHTF was created in order to promote and reconcile prosperity and conservation in English historic towns. Membership of the Forum currently stands at 47 full members. Their recent publication, *Getting it Right - a Guide to Visitor Management in Historic Towns* (EHTF, 1994), is of particular relevance to the theme of this book. The publication emphasises the importance of planning for visitor management, and draws on comparative good practice from many English historic towns and cities.

But comparative good practice is not confined to any one country. Hopefully the research for this book has illustrated the value of Europe-wide comparative studies and the importance of networking on this larger scale in the interest of maintaining and enhancing the heritage of Europe's historic towns and cities. The Europe-wide network which has been established for this study provides a unique framework for dissemination and for further research.

Appendices

Tourism and the Environment
Visitor Impact Management and Cultural Heritage

OXFORD
BROOKES **Shankland Cox** **CISET**
UNIVERSITY Environmental Planning UNIVERSITÀ DEGLI STUDI DI VENEZIA

PLEASE NOTE: We refer to *TOURISTS* in this questionnaire, as both to visitors staying overnight in your town/city (*overnight visitors*) AND those visiting only for the day (*day visitors*)

Town/City: _____ Your Organisation: _____

Contact address and tel: _____

Contact name: _____ Position: _____

What is your specific `tourism' function?: _____

I would be interested/not interested* in attending the experts' workshop (*Please delete as appropriate*)

(Nominees? _____)

BACKGROUND: VISITORS AND ATTRACTIONS

1. What is the approximate current population of your town/city? _____ (_____Date)

2. Approximately how many **Tourists** visit your town/city annually? _____   ☐ Don't Know

    3. What percentage of these *Tourists* are **Overnight Visitors?** ____% **Day Visitors Only?** _____%

4. How many nights, on average, do **Overnight Visitors** stay in your town/city? _____   ☐ Don't Know

5. How many hours, on average, do **Day Visitors** stay in your town/city? _____   ☐ Don't Know

6. Which months do you have the most **Tourists** in your town/city? (*Please state busiest first*)
    _____

    _____

7. On your busiest days, how many Tourists are in your town/city? _____   ☐ Don't Know

8. What are the main reasons for Tourists visiting your town/city? _____
    (*please rank 3, with 1 being the most important reason*)

    ___ business purposes   ___visit the town's historic centre   ___ shopping
    ___ use sporting facilities   ___attend plays, concerts, etc.   ___ educational purposes
    ___ visit specific sites or attractions (please specify) _____
    _____
    ___ other (please specify) _____

9. What are the top 3 tourist attractions in your town/city by visitor volume?
(please only include sites/attractions within the historic centre of your town/city)

Site/Attraction	Peak Tourist Months	Annual Number of Visitors	Measured or Estimated	Peak Daily Average	Estimated Maximum Daily Capacity
1					
2					
3					

10. Who is primarily responsible for tourism management in your town/city?

☐ *Local Government Agency*   ☐ *Commercial Sector Agency*   ☐ *National Government Agency*
☐ *Regional/Provincial Government Agency*   *Other (please specify)_____*

VISITOR IMPACTS AND MANAGEMENT

11. Have `tourism' studies been undertaken on any of the following subjects over the last 10 years?

Local Traffic Surveys	Yes/No	Year _____
Local Parking Surveys	Yes/No	Year _____
Local Tourism Market Research	Yes/No	Year _____
Local Tourism Physical Impact Studies	Yes/No	Year _____
Local Tourism Economic Impact Studies	Yes/No	Year _____
Local Tourism Cultural Impact Studies	Yes/No	Year _____
Other (please specify)_____	Yes/No	Year _____

12. Please circle the number which best indicates your level of agreement (7=high, 1=low) with each of the following statements with regard to your town/city.

	Strongly Agree	Agree	Mildly Agree	Neutral	Mildly Disagree	Disagree	Strongly Disagree
• Most businesses in our town/city serve a tourist market either directly or indirectly	7	6	5	4	3	2	1
• Most businesses would object to measures to reduce tourist numbers in the town/city	7	6	5	4	3	2	1
• Many local residents would like fewer tourists to visit the town/city	7	6	5	4	3	2	1
• Local rents have increased in the town/city because of tourism development	7	6	5	4	3	2	1
• Since tourism development, there are fewer shops directly serving local daily needs	7	6	5	4	3	2	1
• Traditional arts and crafts have been replaced by lower quality products for tourists	7	6	5	4	3	2	1
• Theft has increased with greater tourist numbers	7	6	5	4	3	2	1
• The average spend per tourist has decreased as tourist numbers have increased	7	6	5	4	3	2	1
• Local residents are becoming less tolerant of tourists in the town/city	7	6	5	4	3	2	1
• Personal violence has increased with greater tourist numbers	7	6	5	4	3	2	1

13. Do any of the attractions/sites listed in **Question 9** on the page opposite charge an entrance fee?

	Charge Entrance Fee	If YES, how much?	Currency	Is there a lower fee for local residents?
1.	Yes/No			Yes/No
2.	Yes/No			Yes/No
3.	Yes/No			Yes/No

14. Please circle the number which best describes the problem level of the following issues in your town/city.

	Major Problem	Problematic	Minor Problem	Not a Problem	Don't Know
Lack of attractions to keep tourists longer	4	3	2	1	0
Car parking	4	3	2	1	0
Tourism coach parking	4	3	2	1	0
Traffic congestion	4	3	2	1	0
Crowded pedestrian spaces	4	3	2	1	0
Crowded local shops	4	3	2	1	0
Local air quality	4	3	2	1	0
Erosion/accidental damage to historic sites	4	3	2	1	0
Vandalism caused by tourists	4	3	2	1	0
Local resident dislike of tourism	4	3	2	1	0
Crowding out of local shops/services	4	3	2	1	0
Other (please specify)					

15. How often, if ever, does your office/department receive *complaints from tourists* such as:

	Monthly	Weekly	Daily	Not at all	Don't Know
Not enough/too expensive accommodation	4	3	2	1	0
Nowhere to eat/not enough restaurants	4	3	2	1	0
Can't park in the town/city	4	3	2	1	0
The town is congested with traffic	4	3	2	1	0
Have to wait in line to see attractions	4	3	2	1	0
Streets and/or sites are overcrowded	4	3	2	1	0
Entrance fees are too high	4	3	2	1	0
Can't find tourist information centre	4	3	2	1	0
Other (please specify)					

16. Does your town/city operate any form of specific tourist tax, other than general VAT? ☐ YES ☐ NO

17. If YES, how is this applied or collected?

☐ tourist tax on meals in restaurants   ☐ differential pricing at attractions/facilities
☐ tourist tax on accommodation   ☐ charging for tour coach parking
☐ other (please specify) _____

18. Does your town/city have a published tourism strategy or development plan?   ☐ YES   ☐ NO

19. If YES, what geographic area does it cover?
☐ *Specific Sites and Attractions Only*   ☐ *Historic Town/City Centre Only*
☐ *Whole Town/City*   ☐ *Regional/Provincial Area*   ☐ *Part of National Level Plan*

20. If YES, what are the objectives of this strategy (*please rank order 3 options, 1 being the key objective*)

____ *increase current visitor numbers*   ____ *encourage visitors to come outside the peak season*
____ *reduce current visitor numbers*   ____ *spread visitors throughout the town/city*
____ *better manage current visitors*   ____ *better coordinate local agencies involved in tourism*
____ *increase negative impacts*   ____ *extend the stay of current visitors*
____ *decrease negative impacts*   ____ *spread economic benefits to more local people*
____ *other (please specify)*_____

21. Does your town/city provide and display tourist maps at?: (*please tick as appropriate*)

☐ the train station   ☐ car parks   ☐ tourist coach parks   ☐ airport

22. Are *free* tourist maps available of your town/city?:   ☐ YES   ☐ NO

23. If YES, in what languages are these available?_____

24. Does your town/city have specific tourist signposting to attractions and sites?   ☐ YES   ☐ NO

25. Does your town/city display interpretation panels within the historic centre?   ☐ YES   ☐ NO

26. Is there a tourist information centre in the town/city centre?   ☐ YES   ☐ NO

27. Where is it located?_____ (Please enclose a map with this highlighted)

28. In the tourist peak season, what proportion of daily traffic is tourist related? ____%   ☐ Don't know

29. Approximately what percentage of your tourists arrive in your town/city by:
Private car ____%   Train ____%   Tour coach ____%   Airplane ____%
Other (please specify) _____ ____%

30. Does your town/city have a designated coach drop-off/pick-up point in the town centre?   ☐ YES   ☐ NO

31. Does your town/city have designated tourist coach parks?   ☐ YES   ☐ NO

32. If YES, is there a shuttle bus service from the coach park to the town centre?   ☐ YES   ☐ NO

33. How long does it take to walk from the coach park to the town centre? _____ minutes

34. Does your town/city offer a park and ride bus service?   ☐ YES   ☐ NO

35. Do residents of your town/city pay less for public transport than tourists?   ☐ YES   ☐ NO

36 Is the historic centre of your town/city pedestrianized?   ☐ YES   ☐ NO

OR/ ☐ PARTIALLY (please explain)_____

Thank you very much for taking the time to fill in this questionnaire. Your participation in this research exercise is greatly appreciated. It will make a significant contribution to the Experts' Workshop and the future management of tourism in centres of European Cultural Heritage such as yours.

Good ...., I am undertaking a commissioned survey on the attitudes of local residents to tourism in Oxford. Do you live in Oxford? Are you willing to answer a few questions on this matter? The interview will not take longer than 10 minutes.

A   BACKGROUND INFORMATION

Q1   How long have you lived in Oxford?:

Less than 12 months   ☐
1 - 5 years   ☐
6 - 10 years   ☐
11 - 20 years   ☐

Q2   How much contact (i.e. liaison through work or other activity) do you have with visitors and tourists to Oxford?

None   ☐   Very little   ☐   Some   ☐   Frequent   ☐

Q3   Do you or any members of your household work in the following types of jobs?:

Hotels, Motels, and other   ☐
Accommodation establishments

Restaurants and Catering   ☐

Tourist and Recreation   ☐
Attractions

Transport   ☐

Oxford Colleges   ☐

Entertainment (cinema, theatre,   ☐
concerts, etc.)

None   ☐

B   PERCEPTIONS OF TOURISM

If resident in Oxford for over 10 years go to Q4.
If resident for less than 10 years go to Q5.

Q4.   Do you think the effects of tourism have changed since you moved to Oxford? In what way?

....

....

Q5   What major advantages do you think tourism has brought to Oxford?

....

....

163

Q6   What major _disadvantages_ do you think tourism has brought to Oxford?

....

....

Q7 a.   Do you see tourism as an important local industry in providing _jobs_ for local people?

YES ☐   NO ☐

b.   Do you see tourism as an important local industry in bringing money into Oxford?

YES ☐   NO ☐

Q8   In your opinion, do you think the effect of tourism in Oxford is?:

Good	Neutral	Bad	Don't' know
☐	☐	☐	☐

Q9   Do you think you personally benefit from tourism in any way?

YES ☐   NO ☐

C.   REACTION TO VISITORS

Q10   The following set of statements has been designed to gauge your overall reaction to visitors to Oxford and Oxfordshire. Please indicate which response fits most closely to your opinion. **(Show card 1).**

	D. Disagree **N. Neutral**		**A. Agree**		**DK . Don't Knows**
a	Tourism interferes with residents enjoyment of their own town	D	N	A	DK
b	Tourism brings more money to Oxford than any other types of business or industry	D	N	A	DK
c	Tourists in Oxford erode the local environment and fabric of the City	D	N	A	DK
d	There are better recreation and leisure facilities for local residents because visitors help to support them	D	N	A	DK
e	Tourists using Oxford's local transport system reduces the quality of service provided for local residents	D	N	A	DK
f	Improving and managing tourist facilities in Oxford is money well spent	D	N	A	DK
g	All the different Nationalities amongst visitors to Oxford make the streets more interesting and exciting	D	N	A	DK

164

h	Visitors' interest in Oxford's heritage means that our old buildings are better cared for than otherwise would be	D	N	A	DK
i	Visitors result in unpleasantly overcrowded streets and other out door places	D	N	A	DK
j	Because of tourism, Oxford has a good local transport service (i.e. bus service, taxi service, etc.)	D	N	A	DK
k	Jobs created by tourism are demeaning and of low status	D	N	A	DK
l	Visitors to Oxford interfere with local peoples' use of entertainment, leisure and recreation facilities	D	N	A	DK
m	Visitors to Oxford bring jobs and money and that is more important than the problems they create	D	N	A	DK

Q11   Do you think visitors to Oxford should pay more than local residents to use local facilities paid for by local residents (e.g. swimming, Ice Rink, etc.)?

YES ☐   NO ☐

D.   THE FUTURE

Q12   Do you think that the number of visitors to Oxford is too high, too low, or about right?:

Too High	Too Low	About Right	Don't Know
☐	☐	☐	☐

Q13   National statistics show that Oxford is now the third most visited city in England and the number of visitors to Oxford is increasing. As a local resident are you concerned about this?

YES ☐   NO ☐

Why is that?

....

....

Q14   How should local residents be involved in tourism management and planning (**Select 2**)

Public meetings   ☐

Individuals can object to developments
as they arise attending Council meetings
if they wish   ☐

By surveys from time to time   ☐

By making their views know to
Councillors   ☐

165

By joint discussions with the
tourist industry and planners   ☐

Leave it to the planners   ☐

Other? ....

Q15   What advice would you give to better manage visitors to Oxford?

....

....

....

E.   <u>**DEMOGRAPHIC INFORMATION**</u>

Q16   Can you please indicate which age category you fall into (show card 2).

....

Q17   What is your occupation?

....

Is the respondent:

Male   ☐   Female   ☐

THANK YOU FOR YOUR COOPERATION

References and bibliography

Aldous, T. (1992), 'Managing old towns', *The Planner*, 1 May, p.14.

Anderson, K. and Gayle, F. (eds.) (1992), *Inventing Places: Studies in Cultural Geography*, Longman, Cheshire

Archer, B. (1977), *Tourism Multipliers: the State of the Art*, Bangor Occasional Papers in Economics, No.11, University of Wales, Bangor.

Archer, B. (1982), 'The value of multipliers and their policy implications', *Tourism Management*, Vol.3,No.2, pp.236-241.

Arts Council of Great Britain (1989), *An Urban Renaissance: Sixteen Case Studies Showing the Role of Arts in Urban Regeneration*, Arts Council, London.

Arup (1993), *Environmental Capacity and Development in Historic Cities: A Study with Special Reference to Chester*, Cheshire County Council, Chester.

Ashworth, G. J. (1991), *Heritage Planning: Conservation as the Management of Urban Change*, Geopers, Groningen.

Ashworth, G. J. (1992), Managing Urban Tourism: A Resource Management Crisis in Search of a Resource Management Solution, *Tourism and the City in the 1990s Conference*, CISET, Venice.

Ashworth, G.J. and Tunbridge, J.E. (1990), *The Tourist-Historic City*, Belhaven, London.

Ashworth, G.J. and Goodall, B. (eds.) (1990), *Marketing Tourism Places*, Routledge, London.

Ashworth, G.J. and Voogd, H. (eds.) (1990), *Selling the City: Marketing Approaches in Public Sector Urban Planning*, Belhaven, London.

Atelier, L (1992), *Charleroi: Ville d'Architecture*, Espace Environnement.

Balboni, P., de Marchi, A., Lando, F. and Zanetto, G. (1978), La Percezione dell'Ambiente: L'esperimento di Venezia, Quaderni Ciedart 3, *Edizioni Ciedart*, Venezia.

Barnett, S. (1991), 'Selling us short? Cities, culture and economic development,' in Fisher, M. and Owen, U. (eds.), *Whose Cities?*, Penguin, Harmondsworth.

Becker, R.H., Jubbenville, A, and Burnett, G.W. (1984), 'The search for a social carrying capacity', *Leisure Sciences*, Vol.6, No.4, pp 475-486.

Bianchini, F. (1990), 'The arts and the urban regeneration process,' in MacGregor, S. and Pimlott, P. (eds.), *Tackling the Inner Cities: The 1980's Reviewed, Prospects for the 1990's*, Clarendon Press, Oxford, pp.215-50.

Bianchini, F. (1991), 'Alternative cities,' *Marxism Today*, June, pp.36-8.

Bianchini, F. and Parkinson, M. (1993), *Cultural Policy and Urban Regeneration: The West European Experience*, Manchester University Press, Manchester.

Bianchini, F., Dawson, J. and Evans, R. (1990), *Flagship Projects in Urban Regeneration, Working Paper 16*, Centre for Urban Studies, University of Liverpool.

Bianchini, F., Fisher, M., Montgomery, J. and Worpole, K. (1991), *City Centres, City Cultures: The Role of the Arts in the Revitalisation of Towns and Cities*, Centre for Local Economic Strategies, Manchester.

Bianchini, F. and Schwengal, H. (1991), 'Re-imagining the city' in Corner, S. and Harvey, J. (eds.), *Enterprise and Heritage: Cross Currents in National Culture*, Routledge, London, pp.212-34.

Bishop, J. (1986), *Milton Keynes: The Best of Both Worlds: Public and Professional Views of the New City*, Occasional Paper 24, School for Advanced Urban Studies, University of Bristol.

Bjorklund, E. and Philbrick, A. (1972), 'Spatial configurations of mental processes' in Belanger, M. and Janelle, D. (eds) , in *Building Regions for the Future*, Dept of Geography, Lowal University, Quebec.

Boissevan, J. (1979), 'The impact of tourism on a dependent island, Gozo, Malta', *Annals of Tourism Research*, Vol. 6, No.1, pp.79- 90.

Boorstin, D.J. (1964), *The Image: A Guide to Pseudo-events in America*, Harper Row, New York.

Boyle, M. and Hughes, G. (1991), 'Glasgow's role as European City of Culture', *Area*, Vol. 23, No.2, pp.217-228.

Brackenbury, M. (1993), Towards sustainable Tourism, in *Environment and Development: Newsletter for International Travel and Tourism*, No.2, World Travel and Tourism Environment Research Centre, Oxford Brookes University, Oxford.

Brayley, R. et al (1990) 'Perceived impact of tourism on social issues', *Annals of Tourism Research*, Vol.17, No.2.

Briassoulis, H. and Van der Straaten, J. (eds.) (1992), *Tourism and the Environment*, Kluwer, Dordrecht.

Brotherton, D.I. (1979), 'Ecological Carrying Capacity,' in Wright, S.E. and Buckley, G.P. (eds.), *Ecology and Design in Amenity Land Management*, Recreation Ecology Research Group, Wye College, Ashford, Kent, pp.77-86.

Brown, I. and Fearon, G. (1939), *Amazing Monument: A Short History of the Shakespeare Industry*, Heinemann, London.

Bruce, D. (1993), *A Handbook of Good Practice for Sustainable Tourism in Walled Towns*, Report to Tourism Unit, Directorate General 23, Commission of the European Communities.

Budowski, G. (1976), 'Tourism and conservation: conflict, co-existence or symbiosis', *Environmental Conservation*, Vol.3, No.1, pp.27-31.

Built Environment (Editorial) (1974), 'Tourism: too much of a good thing?', *Built Environment*, August, pp.386-391.

Burgess, J. (1982), 'Selling places: environmental images for the executive,' *Regional Studies*, Vol. 16, pp.1-17.

Burton, R.C.J. (1974), The recreational carrying capacity of the countryside: a research report presenting the methodology and results of ecological and psychological surveys of Cannock Chase, Staffordshire, *Occasional Publication No.11*, Keele University Library, Keele, Staffs.

Bury, R.L. (1976), 'Recreation carrying capacity - hypothesis or reality?', *Parks and Recreation*, January, pp.22-55 and 56-57.

Butler, R.W. (1980), 'The concept of a tourist area cycle of evolution', *Canadian Geographer*, Vol.24, pp.5-12.

Canestrelli, E. and Costa, P. (1991), 'Tourist carrying capacity: a fuzzy approach,' *Annals of Tourism Research*, Vol.18, No.2, pp.295-311.

Cantacuzino, S. (1994), 'Criteria for timeless qualities,' *Building Design*, 22 April, pp.12-13.

Canterbury District Council (1993), 'Tourism', Canterbury District Council (CDC) *Profile*, No.4, March 1993.

Castells, M. (1989), *The Informational City: Information Technology, Economic Restructuring and the Urban-Regional Process*, Blackwell, Oxford.

Castells, M. and Hall, P. (1994), *Technopoles of the World: The Making of 21st Century Industrial Complexes*, Routledge: London.

Cheng, J.R. (1980), 'Tourism: how much is too much?', *Canadian Geographer*, Vol. 24, No.2, pp.72-80.

Cherry, G. (1994), *Birmingham: A Study in Geography, History and Planning*, John Wiley, Chichester.

Civic Trust/English Historic Towns Forum (1993), Traffic Measures in Historic Towns: An Introduction to Good Practice, *Civic Trust/English Historic Towns Forum*, London.

Clark, G., Darrall, J., Grove-White, R., Macnaghten, P. and Urry, J. (1994), *Leisure Landscapes: Leisure, Culture and the English Countryside: Challenges and Conflicts*, Council for the Protection of Rural England and the Centre for the Study of Environmental Change, Lancaster University, Lancaster.

Clarke, A. (1986), 'Local authority planners or frustrated tourism marketeers?' *The Planner*, May, pp.23-26.

Claval, P. (1984), 'Reflections on the Cultural Geography of the European City', in Agnew, J. A., Mercer, J. and Sopher, D. E. (eds.), *The City in Cultural Context*, Allen and Unwin, Boston, pp.29-49.

Clay, G. (1973), 'Epitome Districts,' *Close-Up: How to Read the American City*, Praeger, New York, pp.38-65.

Clifford, S. and King, A. (1993), *Local Distinctiveness. Place, Particularity and Identity*, Common Ground, London.

Cohen, E. (1978), 'The impact of tourism on the physical environment', *Annals of Tourism Research*, Vol.5, No.2, pp.215-37.

Cohen, E. (1979), 'Rethinking the sociology of tourism', *Annals of Tourism Research*, Vol.6, No.1, pp.18-35.

Cohen, N. (1993), 'Renaissance that never was,' *Independent on Sunday* (London), 10 October, p.11.

Cohen, S. (1991), 'Popular music and urban regeneration: the music industries of Merseyside,' *Cultural Studies*, Vol.5, pp.332-346.

Comedia (1991), *Out of Hours*, Comedia, London.

Commission of the European Communities (1985), *On the assessment of the effects of certain public and private projects on the environment*, Official Journal, L175 (5 July 1985).

Commission of the European Communities (1991), *Community Action Plan to Assist Tourism*, CEC, Brussels.

Commission of the European Communities (1991), *Europe 2000: Outlook for the Development of the Community's Territory*, CEC, Directorate General for Regional Policy, Brussels.

Commission of the European Communities (1992), *Towards sustainability: a European Community programme of policy and action in relation to the environment and sustainable development*, Vol.2, CEC, Brussels.

Cooke, K. (1982), 'Guidelines for Socially Appropriate Tourism development in British Columbia,' *Journal of Travel Research*, Vol.21, No.1 pp.22-28.

Cooke, P. (1989), *Localities: the Changing Face of Urban Britain*, Unwin Hyman, London.

Cooper, C., Fletcher, J., Gilbert, D. and Wanhill, S. (1993), *Tourism: Principles and Practice*, Pitman Publishing, London.

Corfield, P.J. (1982), *The Impact of English Towns 1700 - 1800*, Oxford University Press, Oxford.

Corner, J. and Harvey, S. (eds.) (1991), *Enterprise and Heritage: Cross Currents of National Culture*, Routledge, London.

Costa, P. (1990), 'Il Turismo a Venezia e l'Ipotesi Venetiaexpo 2000,' *Politica del Turismo*, Vol.7, No.1, pp.7-24.

Costa, P. (1991), 'Managing tourism carrying capacity of art cities,' *The Tourist Review*, Vol. 4, pp.8-11.

Costa, P. and Van den Borg, J. (1988), 'Um modello lineare per la programmazione del Turismo,' *Turismo a Venezia*, 32/33: pp.21-26.

Costa, P. and Van der Borg, J. (1991), European Art Cities and Flows of Visitors: A Framework for Assessing the Impact of Cultural Tourism, paper to Technical Meeting,' Art Cities and Visitor Flows' Project, *Scuola di Economia del Turismo*, University of Venice, Venice.

Courtauld, S. (1994), 'The heights of folly,' *The Daily Telegraph* (London), 11 June, pp.12-13.

Crawshaw, C. (1993), Tourism and the Environment: Changing Views of Policy and Practice, paper to Councillor's School, *Town and Country Planning Summer School*, Lancaster University, 6 September.

Cummings, J. and Katz, R. (eds.) (1987), *The Patron State: Government and the Arts in Europe, North America and Japan*, Oxford University Press, Oxford.

Curry, B. and Moutinho, L. (1990), *Modelling the Environmental Aspects of Tourism*, University of Wales Press, Cardiff.

Dalibard, J. (1988), 'Can tourist towns be livable?,' *Canadian Heritage*, Vol.14, No.3, pp.3-4.

D'Amore, L.J. (1983), 'Guidelines to planning in harmony with the host community' in Murphy, P.E. (ed), *Tourism in Canada: Selected Issues and Options*, Western Geographical Series, Volume 21, University of Victoria, Victoria B.C., pp.135-160.

Daniels, S. (1992), 'Reconstructing Constable country,' *Geographical Magazine*, Vol.64, October, pp.10-14.

Deasy, G.F. and Griess, P.R. (1966), 'Impact of a tourist facility on its hinterland,' *Annals of the Association of American Geographers*, Vol. 56, June, pp.290-306.

De Bres, Karen (1994), 'Cowtowns or Cathedral precincts? Two models for contemporary urban tourism,' *Area*, Vol.26, No.1, pp.57-67.

De Kadt, E. (1979), *Tourism: Passport to Development?* Oxford University Press, Oxford.

Delevoy, Robert L. et al (1975), *Le Paysage de L'Industrie*, Editions des Archives d'Architecture Moderne, Bruxelles.

Department of the Environment (1989), *Environmental Assessment: A Guide to the Procedures*, HMSO, London.

171

Department of the Environment (1990), Tourism and the Inner City, *DoE Inner City Research Programme*, HMSO, London.

Department of the Environment (1992), *Development Plans and Regional Planning: Planning Policy Guidance Note 12*, HMSO, London.

Department of the Environment (1992), *Tourism: Planning Policy Guidance Note 21*, HMSO, London.

Ditton, R.R., Fedler, A.J. and Graefe, A.R. (1983), 'Factors contributing to perceptions of recreation crowding', *Leisure Sciences*, Vol. 5 No.4 pp.273-288.

Doxey, G.V. (1976), 'When enough's enough: the natives are restless in Old Niagara', *Heritage Canada*, Vol.2, No.2, pp26-7.

Duffield, B. (1982), 'Tourism: the measurement of economic and social impact,' *Tourism Management*, Vol.3, No.4, pp.248-255.

Elwyn Owen, R. et al (1993), 'Sustainable tourism in Wales: from theory to practice', *Tourism Management*, Vol.14, No.6, pp.463-474.

English Historic Towns Forum (1994), *Getting it Right: A Guide to Visitor Management in Historic Towns*, English Historic Towns Forum, English Tourist Board, Donaldsons Chartered Surveyors, Bath.

English Tourist Board (1979), *English Cathedrals and Tourism: Problems and Opportunities*, English Tourist Board, London.

English Tourist Board/ Department of Employment (1991), *Tourism and the Environment: Maintaining the Balance*, English Tourist Board, London.

English Tourist Board/Department of National Heritage (1993), *Tourism and the Environment: Challenges and Choices for the 1990s*, English Tourist Board, London.

Ermolli and Guidotti (1991), 'Un'Ipotesi Progettuale per il Monitoraggio e il Governo dei Flussi Turistici di Venezia,' *La Rivista Veneta*, Vol. 38, pp.103-114.

European Centre for Traditional and Regional Cultures (1988), *Study of the Social, Cultural and Linguistic Impact of Tourism in and upon Wales*, Wales Tourist Board.

Evans, B. (1994), 'Planning, Sustainability and the Chimera of Community,' *Town and Country Planning*, April.

Farrell, B. and Runyan, D. (1991), 'Ecology and Tourism', *Annals of Tourism Research*, Vol.18, pp.26-40.

Fay, S. and Knightly, P. (1976), *The Death of Venice*, Andre Deutsch, London.

Fisher, A.C. and Krutilla, J. (1972), 'Determination of optimal capacity of resource-based recreation facilities,' *Natural Resources Journal*, Vol.12.

Fleet, M. (1994), 'Oxford calls for a ban on spitting,' *The Daily Telegraph* (London), 15 July.

Flemming, R. L. and von Tscharner, R. (1987), *Placemakers: Creating Public Art That Tells You Where You Are*, Harcourt Brace Jovanovich.

Ford, L.R. (1978), 'Continuity and change in historic cities: Bath, Chester and Norwich,' *Geographical Review*, Vol. 68, No. 3, pp.253-73.

Gambuzza (1990), *L'Ambiente del Turismo*, Societa' Veneta Portogruaro, Venice.

Garreau, J. (1991), *Edge City: Life on the New Frontier*, Doubleday, New York.

Getz, D. (1982), 'A rationale and methodology for assessing capacity to absorb tourism,' *Ontario Geography*, No. 19 pp.92-101.

Getz, D. (1983), 'Capacity to absorb tourism: concepts and implications for strategic planning,' *Annals of Tourism Research*, Vol. 10, No.2, pp.239-263.

Getz, D. (1991), *Festivals, Special Events and Tourism*, Van Nostrand Reinhold, New York.

Glasson, J. (1992), *An Introduction to Regional Planning*, UCL Press, London.

Glasson, J. (1994), Oxford: A Heritage City Under Pressure - visitors, impacts and management responses, *Tourism Management*, Vol 15, No 2.

Glasson, J., Godfrey, K.B., Goodey, B., Van der Borg, J. and Absalom, H. (1993), *Approaches to Carrying Capacity and Visitor Management in Areas of Cultural Heritage in Europe*, Report to the Tourism Unit, Directorate General 23, Commission of the European Communities, November.

Glasson, J., Therivel, R. and Chadwick, A. (1994), *An Introduction to Environmental Impact Assessment*, UCL Press, London.

Glasson, J., Thomas, J., Chadwick, A., Elwin, J., Therivel, R., Crawley, R. and Bibbings, L. (1992), *Oxford Visitor Study*, Oxford Centre for Tourism and Leisure Studies (OCTALS), Oxford Brookes University, Oxford.

Globe '90 Tourism Stream Action Strategy Committee (1990), *An Action Strategy for Sustainable Tourism Development*, Tourism Canada, Vancouver.

Godfrey, K.B. (1993), *Tourism and Sustainable Development: Towards a Community Framework*, unpublished PhD dissertation, School of Planning, Oxford Brookes University, Oxford.

Godfrey, K.B. (1994), '*Sustainable tourism: what is it really?*', address to the United Nations Economic Commission for Europe, Human Settlements Division, 18th Meeting of Experts on Human Settlements Problems in the Mediterranean, Nicosia, Cyprus, 6-8 July.

Godfrey, K.B., Goodey, B. and Glasson, J. (1994a), '*Tourism Management in Europe's Historic Cities: Problems and Prospects*', paper presented at the Quality Management in Urban Tourism: Balancing Business and Environment, University of Victoria, Canada, November 10-12.

Godfrey, K.B. (1994b), '*Sustainable Tourism: the conflicts between global policy and local action*', paper presented at the Quality Management in Urban Tourism: Balancing Business and Environment, University of Victoria, Canada, November 10-12.

Godshalk, D.R. and Parker, F.H (1975), 'Carrying capacity: a key to environmental planning', *Journal of Soil and Water Conservation*, Vol. 30, No.4, pp.160-175.

Gold, J.R. and Ward, S.V. (eds)(1994), *Place Promotion: the Use of Publicity and Marketing to Sell Towns and Regions*, John Wiley, Chichester.

Gomme, A. (1964), 'The townscape of tourism,' *The Architectural Review*, Vol. 136 No.810 pp.112-8.

Goodall, B. (1993), 'Industrial heritage and tourism,' *Built Environment*, Vol. 19, No. 2, pp.93-104.

Goodey, B. (1990), *Market Factors in the Production of Heritage Landscapes*, paper presented to the Landscape Research Group Conference, 'Landscape, Heritage and National Identity,' University of Nottingham, 8-9 September.

Goodey, B. (1991), *Drawing the Line on Town Centre Theme Parks?*, paper to ACSP-AESOP Joint International Congress, School of Planning, Oxford Polytechnic, July 8.

Goodey, B. (1992), 'In league with Smigielskiville,' *Town and Country Planning*, June.

Goodey, B. (1993), 'Venice 61, 000 Arsenal 0.' *Town and Country Planning*, July, 191-2.

Goodey, B. (1993a), *Urban Planning and the Hierarchy of Cultural Markets*, paper to Conference 'Financing of Culture in Towns', Council of Europe, Prague, 7-9 October.

Goodey, B. (1993b), 'I've seen the future ...' *Town and Country Planning*, November, 334-5.

Goodey, B. (1993c), 'Urban Design of Central Areas and Beyond,' in Hayward, R. and McGlynn, S. (eds.), *Making Better Places: Urban Design Now*, Butterworth Architecture, Oxford, pp.53-8.

Goodey, B. (1994a), 'History play,' *Town and Country Planning*, April, 103.

Goodey, B. (1994a), 'Spreading the benefits of heritage visitor quarters,' *International Journal of Heritage Studies*, Vol. 1, No.1 Spring, pp.18-29.

Goodey, B. (1994b), 'Art-full places: public art to sell public spaces?' in Gold, J.R. and Ward, S.V. (eds.), *Place Promotion: The Use of Publicity and Marketing to Sell Towns and Regions*, John Wiley, Chichester, 154-79.

Goodey, B. (1994c), 'Selling cultural heritage: conflicts and possibilities,' in Krumbein, W.E., Brimblecombe, Cosgrove, D.E. and Staniforth, S. (eds.), *Durability and Change: The Science, Responsibility and Cost of Sustaining Cultural Heritage*, Chichester, John Wiley.

Graefe, A.R. (1989), 'Social psychological carrying capacity,' *Proceedings of the National Outdoor Recreation Forum*, pp.451-454.

Graefe, A.R., Vaske, J.J. and Kuss, F.R. (1984), 'Social carrying capacity' *Leisure Science*, Vol. 6, No.4.pp.395-431.

Graefe, A.R., Kuss, F.R. and Vaske, J.J. (1987), *Recreation Impacts and Carrying Capacity: A Visitor Impact Management Framework*, review draft, National Parks and Conservation Association, Washington, D.C.

Graefe, A.R., Kuss, F.R. and Vaske, J.J. (1990), *Visitor Impact Management: The Planning Framework*, National Parks and Conservation Association, Washington, D.C.

Griffiths, R. (1993), 'The politics of cultural policy in urban regeneration,' *Policy and Politics*, Vol. 21,pp.39-46.

Hall, C.M. (1992), *Hallmark Tourist Events: Impacts, Management and Planning*, Belhaven, London.

Hall, J.M. (1974), 'The capacity to absorb tourists,' *Built Environment*, Vol. 3 No.8, pp.392-397.

Hamilton, A. (1990), 'The enchanted nightmare,' *The Guardian* (London), 10 August, 21.

Harvey, D. (1987), *The Condition of Postmodernity: An Enquiry into the Origins of Postmodernity*, Blackwell, Oxford.

Harrison, T. (1993) 'Why Capacity?' in English Historic Towns Forum (eds), *Environmental Capacity and Development in Historic Towns*, EHTF, Bath.

Haukeland, J. (1984), 'Socio-cultural impacts of tourism in Scandinavia: studies of three host communities', *Tourism Management*, Vol.5, No.3, pp.207-214.

Heidelberg, City of (1993), *Guidelines on Tourism Heidelberg*, Heidelberg.

Hendee, J.C., Stankey, G.H. and Lucas, R.C. (1990), *Wilderness Management*, 2nd edn., North American Press, Golden, Colorado.

Hewison, R. (1987), *The Heritage Industry: Britain in a Climate of Decline*, Methuen, London.

Hindley, G. (1983), *Tourists, Travellers and Pilgrims*, Hutchinson, London.

Hobsbawm, E. and Ranger, T. (eds.) (1983), *The Invention of Tradition*, Cambridge University Press, Cambridge.

Insall, D. (1968), *Chester - A Study in Conservation*, HMSO, London.

Inskeep, E. (1987), 'Environmental Planning for Tourism', *Annals of Tourism Research*, Vol.14, No.1, pp.118-135.

International Institute for Sustainable Development (1993), *'Indicators for sustainable management of tourism: report of the international working group on indicators of sustainable tourism to the Environment Committee'*, World Tourism Organisation: Madrid.

Jackson. I. (1986), 'Carrying capacity for tourism in small tropical Caribbean Islands', *UNEP Industry and Environment*, January - March, pp.7-10.

Jakle, J.A. (1983), 'Images of place: symbolism and the Middle Western Metropolis,' in Patton, C. and Checkoway, B. (eds.), *The Metropolitan Midwest*, University of Illinois Press, Urbana.

175

Jakle, J.A. (1985), *The Tourist: Travel in Twentieth-Century North America*, University of Nebraska Press, Lincoln.

Jansen-Verbeke, M. (1986), 'Inner city tourism: resources, tourists, promoters,' *Annals of Tourism Research*, Vol.13, No.1, pp.79-100.

Jansen-Verbecke, M.C. (1990), 'Fun shopping: a challenge to planning,' in Ashworth, G.J. and Goodall, B. (eds.), *Marketing Tourism Places*, Routledge, London.

Jansen-Verbeke, M.C. (1991), *Managing and Monitoring the Tourism Carrying Capacity in a Historical City: The Planning Issues*, AESOP Congress: Oxford.

Jarvis, B. (1987), 'The next best thing to being there: the environmental rhetoric of advertising,' *Landscape Research*, Vol. 12, No.3, pp.14-19.

Johnson, D.A.and Schaffer, D. (eds.)(1994), 'The rusting of the sunbelt,' *Built Environment* (Issue), Vol.20, No.1.

Johnson, P.S. and Thomas, R.B. (1992), *Tourism, Museums and the Local Economy*, Edward Elgar, Aldershot.

Johnson, P.S. and Thomas, R.B. (1994), 'The notion of "capacity" in tourism: a review of the issues' in Cooper, C.P. and Lockwood, A. (eds), *Progress in Tourism, Recreation and Hospitality Management*, Vol. 5, John Wiley, Chichester, pp.297-308.

Judd, D. and Parkinson, M. (eds.) (1990), *Leadership and Urban Regeneration: Cities in North America and Europe*, Sage, London.

Kearns, G. and Philo, C. (eds.) (1993), *Selling Places*, Pergamon, Oxford.

Keating, M. (1988), *The City That Refused to Die*, Aberdeen University Press, Aberdeen.

Keith, M. and Pile S. (eds.) (1993), *Place and the Politics of Identity*, Routledge, London.

Krippendorf, J. (1987), *The Holiday Makers*, Heinemann, London.

Krippendorf, J. (1993), 'Impacts of Tourism on the Environment', in English Tourist Board/Department of National Heritage, *Tourism and the Environment: Challenges and Choices for the 1990s*, English Tourist Board, London.

Kuss, F.R., Graefe, A.R. and Vaske, J.J. (1990), *Visitor Impact Management: A Review of Research*, Vol.1, National Parks and Conservation Association: Washington, D.C.

Larkham, P.J. (1990), 'Conservation and the management of historical townscapes', in Slater, T.R. (ed.), *The Built Form of Western Cities*, Leicester University Press, Leicester, pp.349-69.

Law, C.M. (1992), 'Urban tourism and its contribution to economic regeneration,' *Urban Studies*, Vol. 29, Nos. 3-4, pp.597-616.

Law, C.M. (1993), *Urban Tourism: Attracting Visitors to Large Cities*, London: Mansell.

Le Goff, J. and Guieysse, L. (1985), *Crise de l'urbain: Futur de la ville*, Economica, Paris.

Leicester City Council (1993), *The Quality of Leicester*, City Council, Leicester.

Leighton, D. (1985), 'Banff today: struggling to cope with success', *Canadian Geographic*, Vol.105, No.1, pp 16-21.

Leinberger, C.B. (1988), 'The six types of urban village cores,' *Urban Land*, Vol. 47, May.

Ley, D. and Olds, K. (1988), 'Landscape as spectacle: World's Fairs and the culture of heroic consumption,' *Environment and Planning D. Society and Space* Vol.6, pp 191-212.

Lichty, R.W. and Steinnes, D.N. (1982), 'Measuring the impact of tourism on a small community', *Growth and Change*, Vol. 13, No.2 pp 36-39.

Lim, H. (1993), 'Cultural strategies for revitalising the city: a review and evaluation,' *Regional Studies*, Vol. 27, No.6 pp.589-595.

Lime, D.W. and Stankey, G.H. (1971), 'Carrying capacity: maintaining outdoor recreation quality', *Proceedings 1971 Forest Recreation Symposium*, Syracuse, New York, pp.174-184.

Lindsay, J.J. (1986), 'Carrying capacity for tourism development in national parks of the United States,' *UNEP Industry and Environment*, January - March, pp.17-20.

Loftman, P., Middleton, A. and Nevin, B. (1994), *Inter-City Competition, Place Promotion and Social Justice, Research Paper 13*, Faculty of the Built Environment, University of Central England in Birmingham.

Lowenthal,D. (1985), *The Past is a Foreign Country*, Cambridge University Press, Cambridge.

Lowenthal, D. and Binney, M. (eds.) (1981), *Our Past Before Us: Why Do We Save It?*, Temple Smith, London.

Lumley, R. (1988), *The Museum Time Machine*, Routledge, London.

Lundgren, (1982),'The tourist frontier of Nouveau Quebec: functions and regional linkages', *Tourist Review*, Vol.57, No.2, pp.10-16.

Lynch, K. (1981), *Good City Form*, The M.I.T. Press, Cambridge, Ma.

MacCannell, D. (1976), *The Tourist: A New Theory of the Leisure Class*, Macmillan, London.

MacCannell, D. (1992). *Empty Meeting Grounds: the Tourist Papers*, Routledge, London.

McCool, S.F. (1991), 'Limits of acceptable change: a strategy for managing the effects of nature-dependent tourism development', paper presented at the *Tourism and the Land: Building a Common Future conference*, December 1-3, Whistler, B.C.

Mace, R. (1976), *Trafalgar Square: Emblem of Empire*, Lawrence and Wishart, London.

McPheters, L. and Stronge, W. (1974), 'Crime as an environmental externality of tourism: Florida,' *Land Economics*, Vol.50, pp.288-292.

Magnus, D. (1992), *Art & Nature Landscapes*, Goethe-Institute and German Commission for UNESCO, Munich.

Manente, and Rizzi (1993), *I Flussi Turistici a Venezia 1989 - 1992*, Working Paper, Department of Economics, University of Venice, Venice.

Martin, B.S. and Uysal, M. (1990), 'An examination of the relationship between carrying capacity and the tourism lifecycle: management and policy implications', *Journal of Environmental Management*, Vol. 31 No.4, pp.327-333.

Mathieson, A. and Wall, G. (1982), *Tourism: Economic, Physical and Social Impacts*, Longman Scientific and Technical: Harlow.

Middleton, V. and Hawkins, R. (1994), Practical Environmental Policies in Travel and Tourism - Part 2, *Travel and Tourism Analyst, No.1*, Economist Intelligence Unit, London.

Montgomery, J. (1990), 'Cities and the art of cultural planning,' *Planning Practice and Research*, Vol.5, No.3, Winter.

Moore, R. (1993), 'A new York, but not a better one,' *The Independent* (London), 7 July.

Morris, James (1983), *Venice*, Faber & Faber, London.

Mossetto, G. (1991), *The Economy of the Cities of Art: A Tale of Two Cities*, Nota di lavoro 91.10, Department of Economics, University of Venice, Venice.

Muller, Peter O. (1986), 'Transportation and urban form: stages in the spatial evolution of the American metropolis,' in Hanson, Sue (ed.), *Geography of Urban Transportation*, Guilford Press, New York.

Mumford, Lewis (1938), *The Culture of Cities*, Secker and Warburg, London.

Murphy, P.E. (1985), *Tourism - A Community Approach*, Methuen: New York.

Myerscough, J. (1988), *The Economic Importance of the Arts in Britain*, Policy Studies Institute, London.

Myerson, J. (1994), 'Talking Shop,' *Times Higher*, 3 June, p. 19.

Nairn, I. and Browne, K. (1963), 'Cathedral Cities,' *The Architectural Review*, September.

Nelson, J.G., Butler, R.W. and Wall, G. (eds) (1993), *Tourism and Sustainable Development: Monitoring, Planning, Managing*, Geography Publication Series Number 37, University of Waterloo, Canada.

Netzer, D. (1992), *Tourism and the City*, Urban Research Center, Robert F. Wagner Graduate School of Public Service, New York University, New York.

Nicholson-Lord, D. (1990), 'Death by tourism,' *The Independent on Sunday* (London), 5 August, pp.3-6.

NRIT (1983), *Heritage Tourist Goods: A Study of the Significance of Monuments and Ancient Buildings and Museums in the Netherlands for Tourism and the Economy*, National Institute of Tourism, Breda.

O'Reilly, A.M. (1986), 'Tourism carrying capacity: concepts and issues,' *Tourism Management*, pp.254-258.

Olsen, D. (1986), *The City as a Work of Art: London, Paris, Vienna*, Yale University Press, New Haven, Conn.

Organisation for Economic Co-operation and Development (1980), *The Impact of Tourism on the Environment*, OECD.

Ousby, Ian (1990), *The Englishman's England: Taste, Travel and the Rise of Tourism*, Cambridge University Press, Cambridge.

Oxford City Council (1992), *Oxford Local Plan Review*. Oxford City Council, Oxford.

Oxfordshire County Council (1992), *Oxfordshire Environmental Audit*, Oxfordshire County Council, Oxford.

Page, S. (1992), 'Tourism planning: managing tourism in a small historic town,' *Town and Country Planning*, July/August, pp.208-11.

Parkin, I., Middleton, P. and Beswick, V. (1989), 'Managing the town and city for visitors and local people,' in Uzzell, D. (ed.), *Heritage Interpretation: The Visitor Experience*, Belhaven, London, pp.108-114.

Pearce, D (1989), *Tourist Development*, Longman, Harlow.

Pearce, D.W. (1992), *Towards sustainable development through environmental assessment*, Working Paper PA92-11, Centre for Social and Economic Reserch in the Global Environment, University College London.

Peterson, R.A. (1990), 'Designing cities without designing buildings?,' *Urban Design Quarterly*, April, pp.6-11.

Pizam, A. (1978), 'Tourism's impacts: the social costs to the destination as perceived by its residents,' *Journal of Travel Research*, Vol.16, pp.8-12.

Prentice, R. (1993), *Tourism and Heritage Attractions*, Routledge, London.

Prentice, R. (1993), 'Assessing the linguistic dimension in the perception of tourism impacts by residents of a tourist destination: a case study of Porthmadog, Gwynedd', *Tourism Management*, Vol.13.

Prentice, R. (1994), 'Heritage: a key sector of the "new" tourism', in Cooper, C.P. and Lockwood, A. (eds.) *Progress in Tourism, Recreation and Hospitality Management*, Vol. 5, John Wiley, Chichester, pp.309-324.

Prentice, R. et al (1994), 'The endearment behaviour of tourists through their interaction with the host community', *Tourism Management*, Vol.15, No.2, pp.126-136.

Reeve, A. (1993), 'Urban design in the absence of community,' in *Urban Design and the Dual City: Responses to the Globalisation of Investment in the Late-Capitalist City*, Joint Centre for Urban Design, Oxford Brookes University, pp.4-9.

Ring, D. (ed.) (1993), *The Urban Prairie*, Mendel Art Gallery/Fifth House Publishers, Saskatoon.

Rispoli, J. and Van der Borg, J. (1988), 'Piu 'Vicini, piu 'Cari', *CoSES Informazioni*, 32/33, pp.57-64.

Roberts, M., Marsh, C. and Salter, M. (1993), *Public Art in Private Places: Commercial Benefits and Public Policy*, University of Westminster Press, London.

Roebuck, S. (1994), 'Calculating Capacity: Chester', *Planning Week*, June, pp.14-15.

Romeril, M. (1989), 'Tourism: the environmental dimension' in Cooper, C. (ed) *Progress in Tourism, Recreation and Hospitality Management*, Belhaven Press, London, PP.103-113.

Salvadori, A (1969), *101 Buildings to See in Venice*, Icon/Harper & Row, New York.

Schmidhauser, H. (1991), 'Summary findings AIEST Congress - Sustainable Tourism Development', *Revue de Tourisme*, Vol. 4.

Schneider, D.M., Godschalk, D.R. and Axler, N. (1978), *The Carrying Capacity Concept as a Planning Tool*, American Planning Association, Planning Advisory Service Report No. 338, Chicago, Ill.

Shelby, B. and Heberlein, T.A. (1984), 'A conceptual framework for carrying capacity determination,' *Leisure Sciences*, Vol. 6 No.4 pp.433-451.

Shelby, B. and Heberlein, T.A. (1986), *Carrying Capacity in Recreational Settings*, Oregon State University Press, Corvallis, Oregon.

Sidaway, R. (1991), *Good Conservation Practice for Sport and Recreation*, Study 37, The Sports Council, Countryside Commission, Nature Conservancy Council, UK and World Wide Fund for Nature, London.

Sjoberg, G. (1965), 'The origin and evolution of cities,' in Scientific American (ed.), *Cities*, Alfred A. Knopf, New York, pp.25-39

Smith, N. and Williams, P. (eds.) (1986), *Gentrification of the City*, Unwin Hyman, London.

Smith, V.L. (1977), *Hosts and Guests: The Anthropology of Tourism*, Blackwell, Oxford.

Smith, V.L. and Eadington, W.R. (eds) (1992), *Tourism Alternatives: Potential and Problems in the Development of Tourism*, University of Pennsylvania Press, Philadelphia.

Smyth, H. (1994), *Marketing the City: The Role of Flagship Developments in Urban Regeneration*, Spon, London.

Snedcof, H. (ed.) (1985), *Cultural Facilities in Mixed Use Development*, The Urban Land Institute, Washington, D.C.

Somerville, C. (1994), 'Bell, book and padlock,' *The Daily Telegraph* Weekend, 9 April, pp.1.

Stankey, G.H. and McCool, S.F. (1984), 'Carrying capacity in recreational settings: evolution, appraisal and application', *Leisure Sciences*, Vol. 6, pp.453-474.

Stankey, G.H., McCool, S.F. and Stokes, G.L. (1984), 'Limits of acceptable change: a new framework for managing Bob Marshal Wilderness Complex', *Western Wildlands*, Vol 103, No.3, pp.33-37.

Stankey, G.H., Cole, D.N., Lucas, R.C., Peterson, M.E. and Frissell, S.S. (1985), *The Limits of Acceptable Change (LAC) System for Wilderness Planning*, USDA Forest Service General Technical Report INT-176, Intermountain Forest and Range Experiment Station, Ogden, Utah.

Swyngedouw, E. (1989), 'The heart of the place: the resurrection of locality in an age of hyperspace,' *Geografisker Annaler*, Vol. 71B, pp.31-42.

Therivel, R. et al (1992), *Strategic ʿEnvironmental Assessment*, Earthscan, London.

Townsend, W (1952), 'Canterbury,' in Molony, E. (ed.), *Portrait of Towns*, Dennis Dobson, London, pp.47-57.

Turner, L. and Ash, J. (1975), *The Golden Horde: International Tourism and the Pleasure Periphery*, Constable, London.

Turner, R.K. and Pearce, D.W. (1992), *Sustainable development: ethics and economics*, Working Paper PA92-09, Centre for Social and Economic Research in the Global Environment, University College London.

United Nations, World Commission on Environment and Development (1987), *Our Common Future*, Oxford University Press, Oxford.

United Nations Conference on Environment and Development (UNCED)(1992), *Agenda 21*, UNCED, Rio de Janerio.

Urry, J. (1990), *The Tourist Gaze: Leisure and Travel in Contemporary Societies*, Sage, London.

Van Beetz, F.P. et.al. (1989), *Cities and Culture, Spatial Reconnaissances 1988* Chapter 1, National Physical Planning Agency, The Hague.

Van den Berg, L., Van der Borg, J. and Van der Meer, J. (1992), *Upcoming Destinations of Urban Tourism: Summary*, paper, European Institute for Comparative Urban Research, Erasmus University, Rotterdam.

Van der Borg, J. (1991), *Tourism and Urban Development: the Case of Venice*, Thesis Publishers, Amsterdam.

Van der Borg, J. (1992), 'Tourism and urban development: the case of Venice, Italy,' *Tourism Recreation Research*, Vol.17, No.2, pp.46-56

Van der Borg, J. (1992), The Management of Tourism in Cities of Art, paper, CISET/EURICUR, Venice/Rotterdam.

Van der Borg, J., Costa, P. and Manente, M. (1992), *Traditional Tourism Cities: Problems and Perspectives: Summary*, paper, Centro Internazionale di Studi sull'Economia Turistica (CISET), Venice.

Vance, James E. (1977), *This Scene of Man: The Role and Structure of the City in the Geography of Western Civization*, Harper's College Press, New York.

Veal, A.J. (1973), *Perceptual Capacity: A Discussion and Some Research Proposals*, Working Paper No.1, Centre for Urban and Regional Studies, University of Birmingham, Birmingham.

Vergo, Peter (ed.) (1989), *The New Museology*, Reaktion Books, London.

Vetter, F. (ed.)(1985), *Big City Tourism*, Reimer Verlag, Berlin.

Vulliamy, E (1992), 'Sights for sore eyes', *Guardian*, October 21, 1992.

Wager, J.A. (1964), *The Carrying Capacity of Wildlands for Recreation*, Forest Service Monograph 2, Society of American Foresters.

Wall, G. (1982), 'Cycles and capacity: incipient theory or conceptual contradiction?', *Tourism Management*, Vol. 3, September, pp.188-192.

Wallace, G.N. (1992), 'Visitor management: lessons form Galapagos National Park' in Lindberg, K. and Hawkins, D.E. (eds), *Ecotourism: a guide for planners and managers*, The Ecotourism Society, North Bennington, Vermont, pp.55-81.

Walsh, K. (1992), *The Representation of the Past: Museums and Heritage in the Post-Modern World*, Routledge: London.

Washburne, R.F. (1982), 'Wilderness Recreational Carrying Capacity: Are Numbers Necessary?', *Journal of Forestry*, Vol.80, pp.726-728.

Wathern, P. (ed) (1988), *Environmental Impact Assessment: Theory and Practice*, Unwin Hyman, London.

Watson, S. (1991), 'Gilding the smokestacks: the new symbolic representations of deindustrialised regions' *Environment and Planning D: Society and Space*, Vol. 9 pp.59-70.

Westlake, T. and White, A. (1992), 'Venice - suffering city of tourist dreams,' *Town and Country Planning*, July/August, pp.210-211.

Whitehand, J.W.R. (1967), 'Fringe belts: a neglected aspect of urban geography,' *Transactions of Institute of British Geographers*, Vol.41, pp.223-233.

Wight, P.A. (1994), *'Limits of Acceptable Change: a recreational-tourism tool in cumulative effects assessement'*, paper presented at the National Conference of the Canadian Society of Environmental Biologists, 13-14 April, Calagary Alberta.

Williams, A. and Shaw, G. (1988b) 'Tourism: candyfloss industry or job generator?' *Town Planning Review*, Vol.59, No.1, pp.81-103.

Williams, P.W. and Gill, A. (1991), *Carrying Capacity Management in Tourism Settings: A Tourism Growth Management Process*, Centre for Tourism Policy and Research, Simon Fraser University, Vancouver, B.C.

Williams, P.W. and Gill, A. (1994), 'Tourism Carrying Capacity Management Issues' in Theabold, W (ed), *Global Tourism: The Next Decade*, Oxford: Butterworth-Heinemann, pp.174-187.

WTO (1983a), *Risks of Saturation or Tourist Carrying Capacity Overload in Holiday Destinations*, PG(IV) B.4.2.2, World Tourism Organisation: Madrid.

WTO (1983b), *Study on tourism's contribution to protecting the Environment*, PG(IV) B.4.2.1, World Tourism Organisation: Madrid.

WTO (1983c), *The Framework of the State's Responsibility for the Management of Tourism*, PG(IV) B.1.4, World Tourism Organisation: Madrid.

WTO (1985a), *The state's role in protecting and promoting culture as a factor of tourism development and the proper use and exploitation of the national cultural heritage of sites and monuments for tourism*, PG(V) B.4.2, World Tourism Organisation: Madrid.

WTO (1985b), 'The risks of saturation or carrying capacity overload in holiday destinations in Europe,' *World Travel*, No. 185: 87-92.

WTO (1985c), *Identification and Evaluation of Those Components of Tourism Services Which Have a Bearing on Tourist Satisfaction and Which can be Regulated, and State Measures to Ensure Adequate Quality of Tourism Services*, PG(V) B.2.2, World Tourism Organisation: Madrid.

WTO (1993), *Yearbook of Tourism Statistics*, WTO, Madrid.

World Travel and Tourism Council (WTTC)(1993), *Travel and Tourism - Complete Edition*, WTTC, Brussels.

World Travel and Tourism Environment Research Centre (WTTERC)(1993, 1994), *World Travel and Tourism Environment Annual Review*, WTTERC, Oxford Brookes University, Oxford.

Wright, P. (1985), *On Living in an Old Country*, Verso, London.

Yale, P. (1991), *From Tourist Attractions to Heritage Tourism*, ELM Publication, Kings Ripton.

Zonn, L. (ed.) (1990), *Place Images in Media*, Rowman and Littlefield, Maryland.

Index

189